South Carolina

impressions

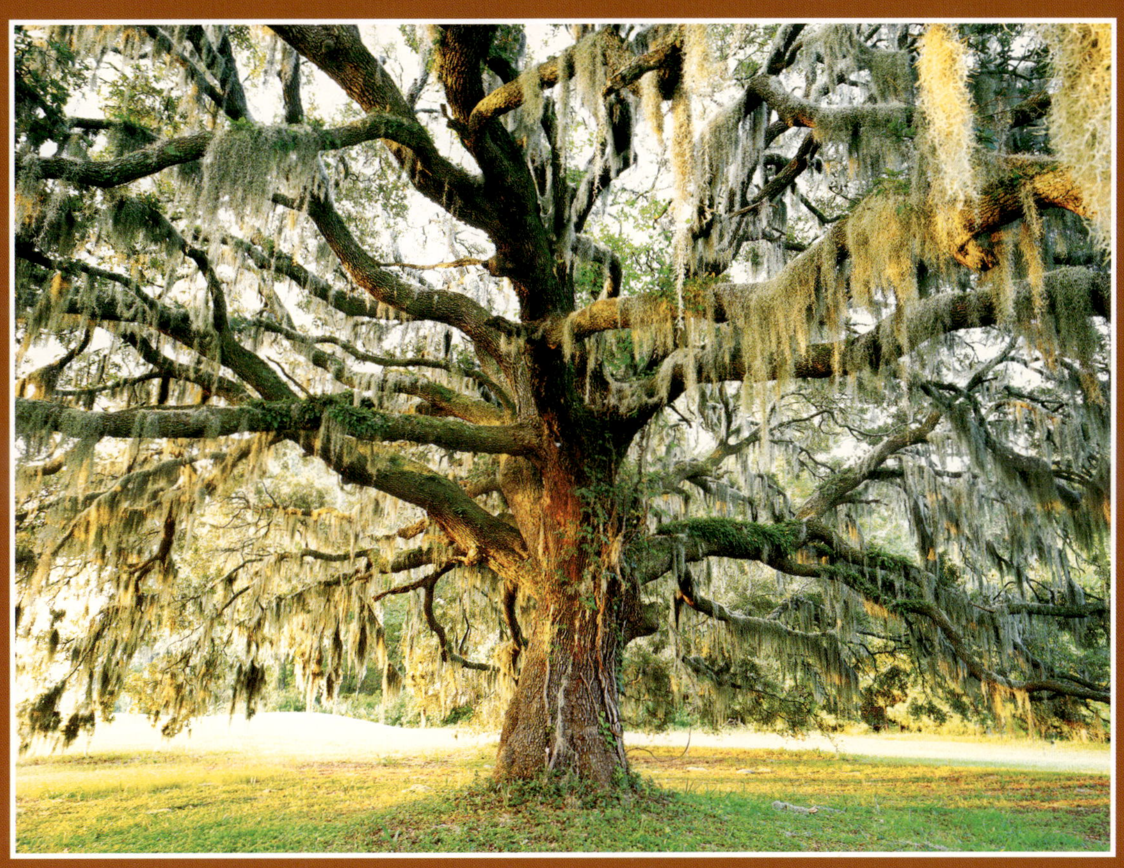

PHOTOGRAPHY BY RON ANDERSON AND ERIC HORAN

South Carolina
impressions

Right: Inviting stretches of white sand lure many a vacationer to Folly Field Beach on Hilton Head Island, the second-largest barrier island on the East Coast. RON ANDERSON

Title page: Sunlight silhouettes a live oak, a symbol of the South. ERIC HORAN

Front cover: Completed in 1742, Charleston's Drayton Hall is the oldest preserved plantation house in the U.S. open to the public. ERIC HORAN

Back cover: A starfish lies on the beach at the Isle of Palms. RON ANDERSON

ISBN 13: 978-1-56037-343-8
ISBN 10: 1-56037-343-1
 For more information on our books write: Farcountry Press, P.O. Box 5630, Helena, MT 59604; call (800) 821-3874; or visit www.farcountry-press.com.

Created, produced, and designed in the United States.
Printed in China.

10 9 8 7 6 1 2 3 4 5

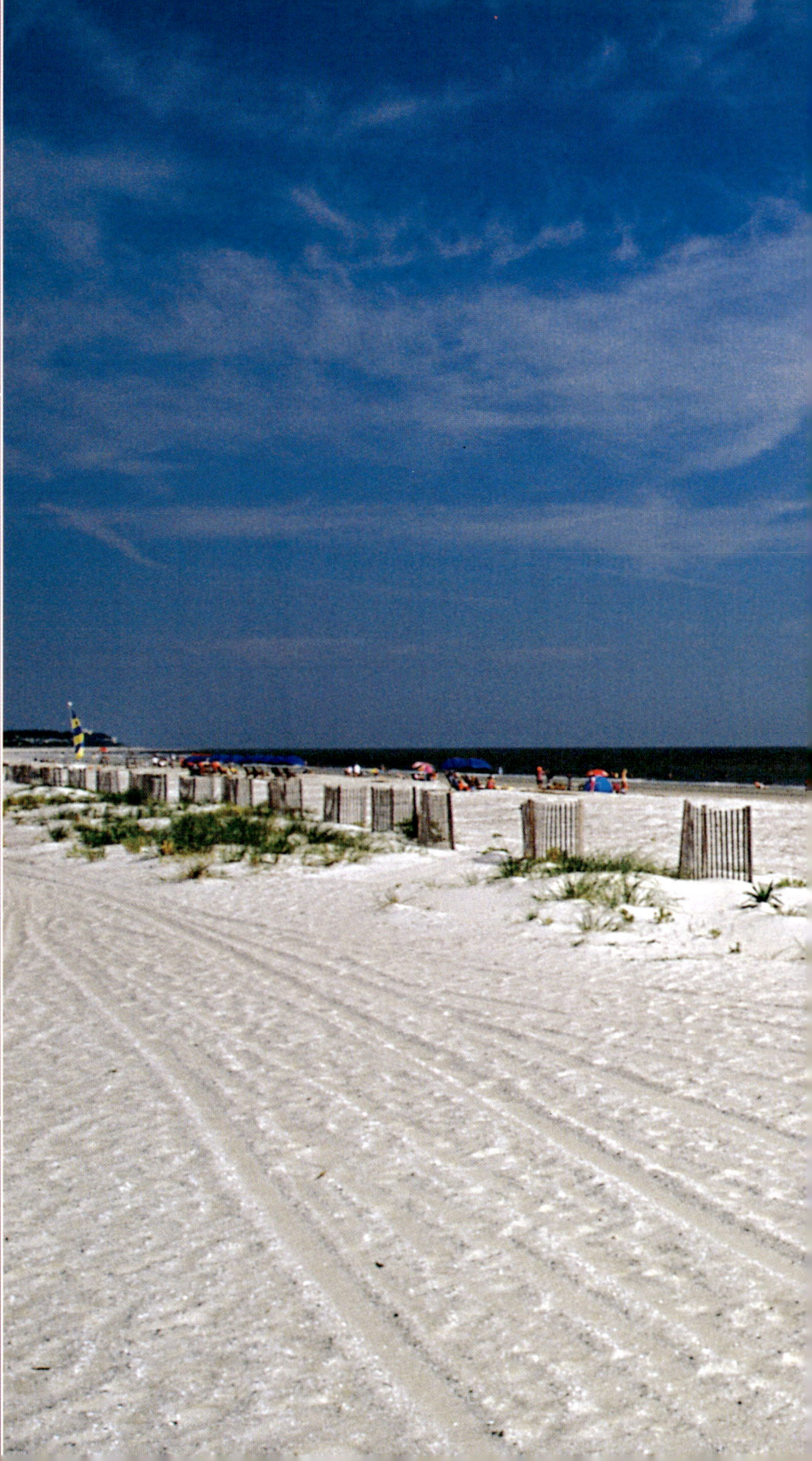

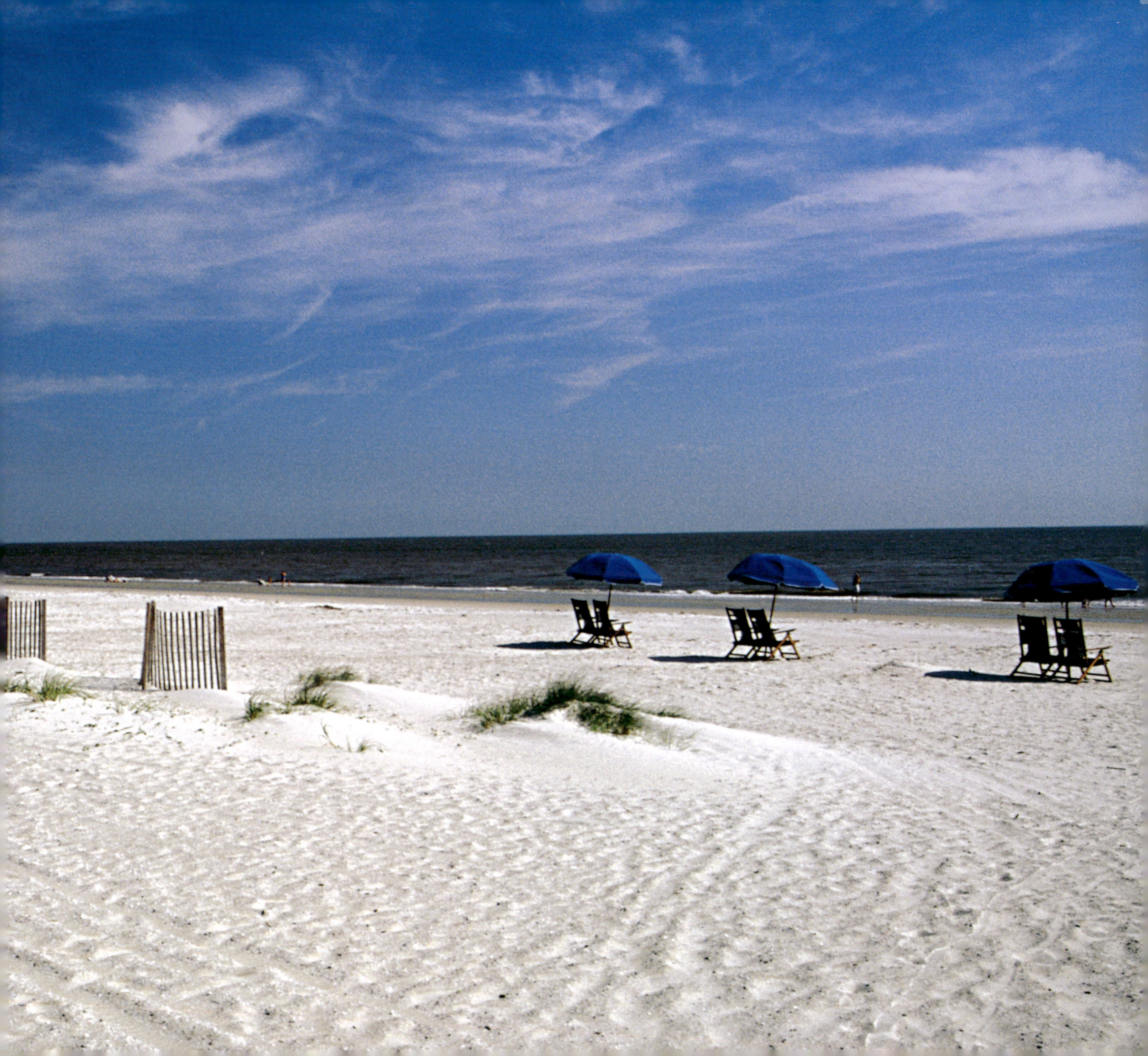

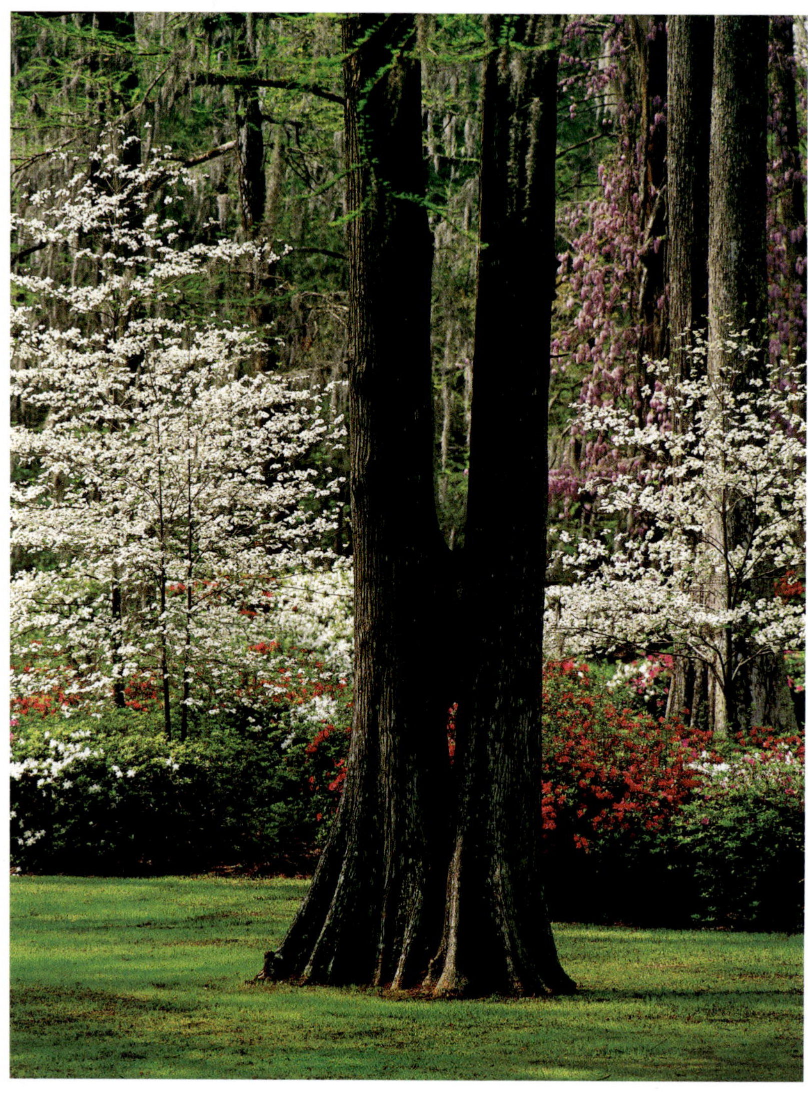

Today Edisto Memorial Gardens is a place of serenity and beauty. But in 1865 a small force of Confederates gathered on the site to defend the Edisto River Bridge. Although the soldiers temporarily halted the advance of the Union Army, eventually they were forced to retreat to Columbia. ERIC HORAN

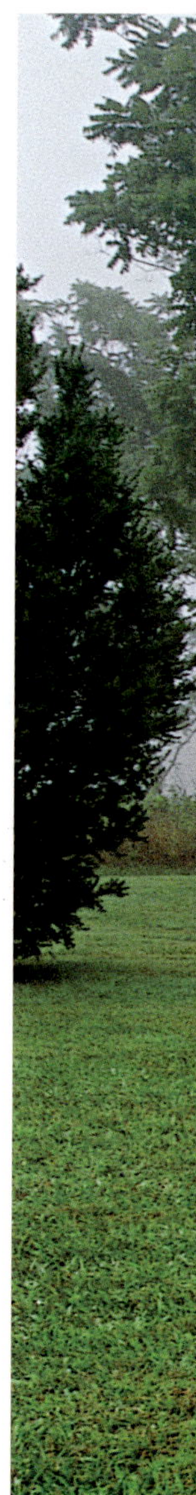

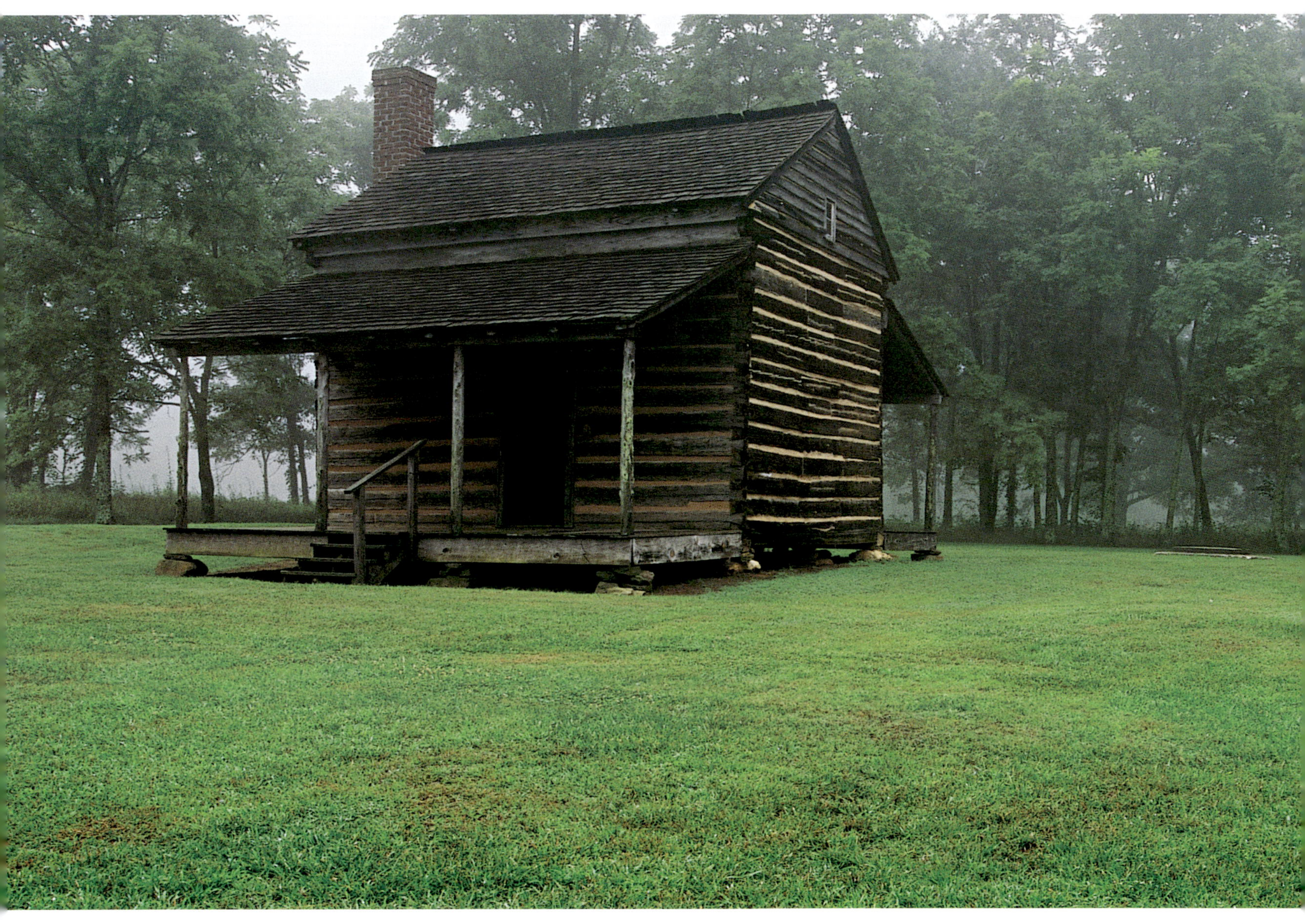

The Robert Scruggs House at Cowpens National Battlefield marks the area where a Patriot force under Brigadier General Daniel Morgan defeated British Army troops commanded by Lieutenant Colonel Banastre Tarleton on the morning of January 17, 1781. The Patriot victory at the Battle of Cowpens was a major link in the chain of events that led to the British surrender at Yorktown, Virginia, the following October, which ended the Revolutionary War. Ron Anderson

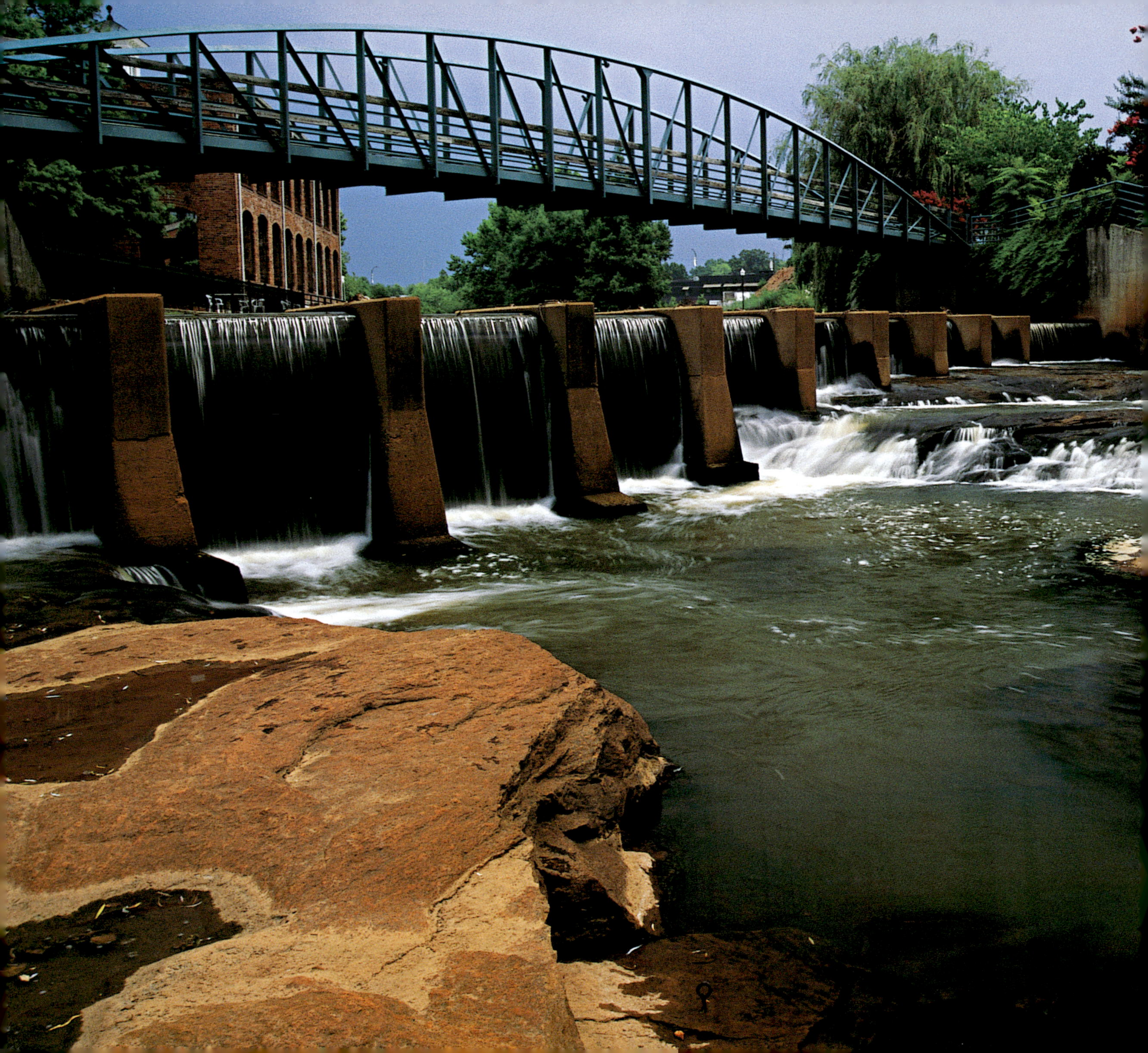

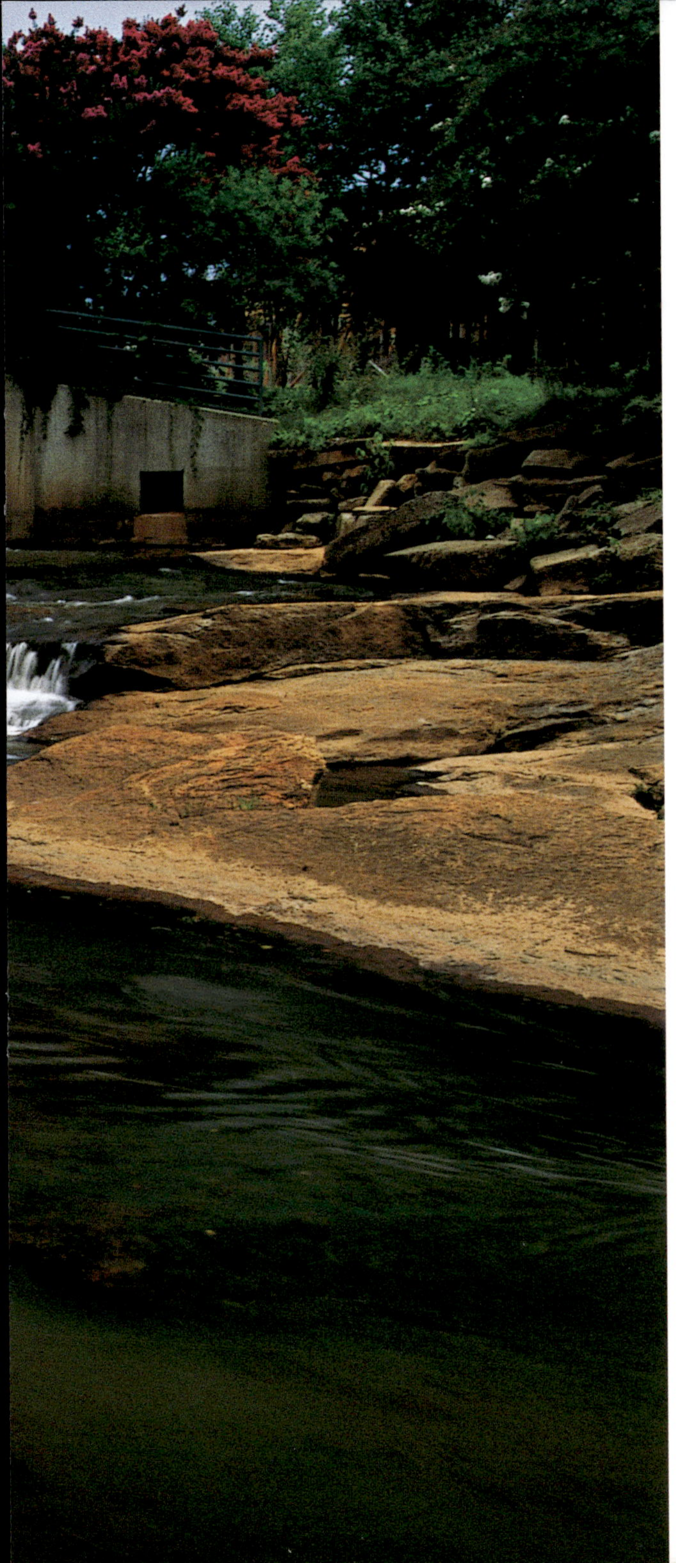

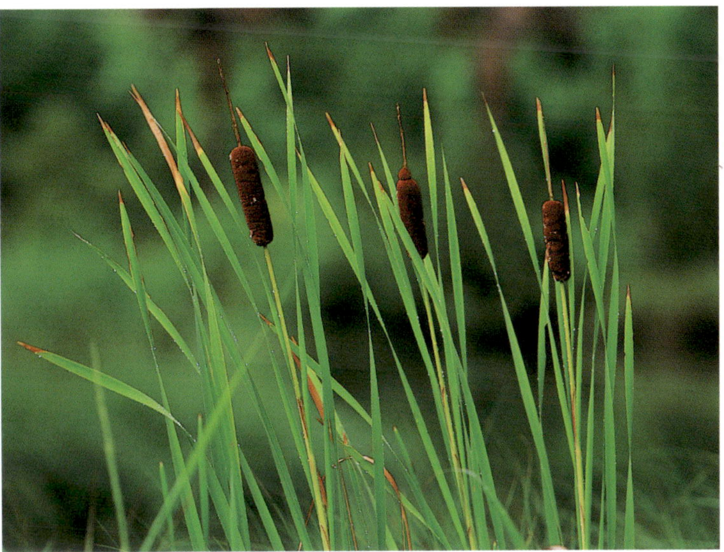

Above: Named for the tribe of Native Americans who inhabited the area until the 1600s, Kiawah Island boasts a wide variety of coastal vegetation, including maritime forest, wilderness swamps, and pristine beaches. ERIC HORAN

Left: The modern Reedy River Bridge spans the Reedy River in downtown Greenville. Located in the northwestern corner of the state, Greenville enjoys a temperate climate and proximity to the attractions of the Blue Ridge Mountains. RON ANDERSON

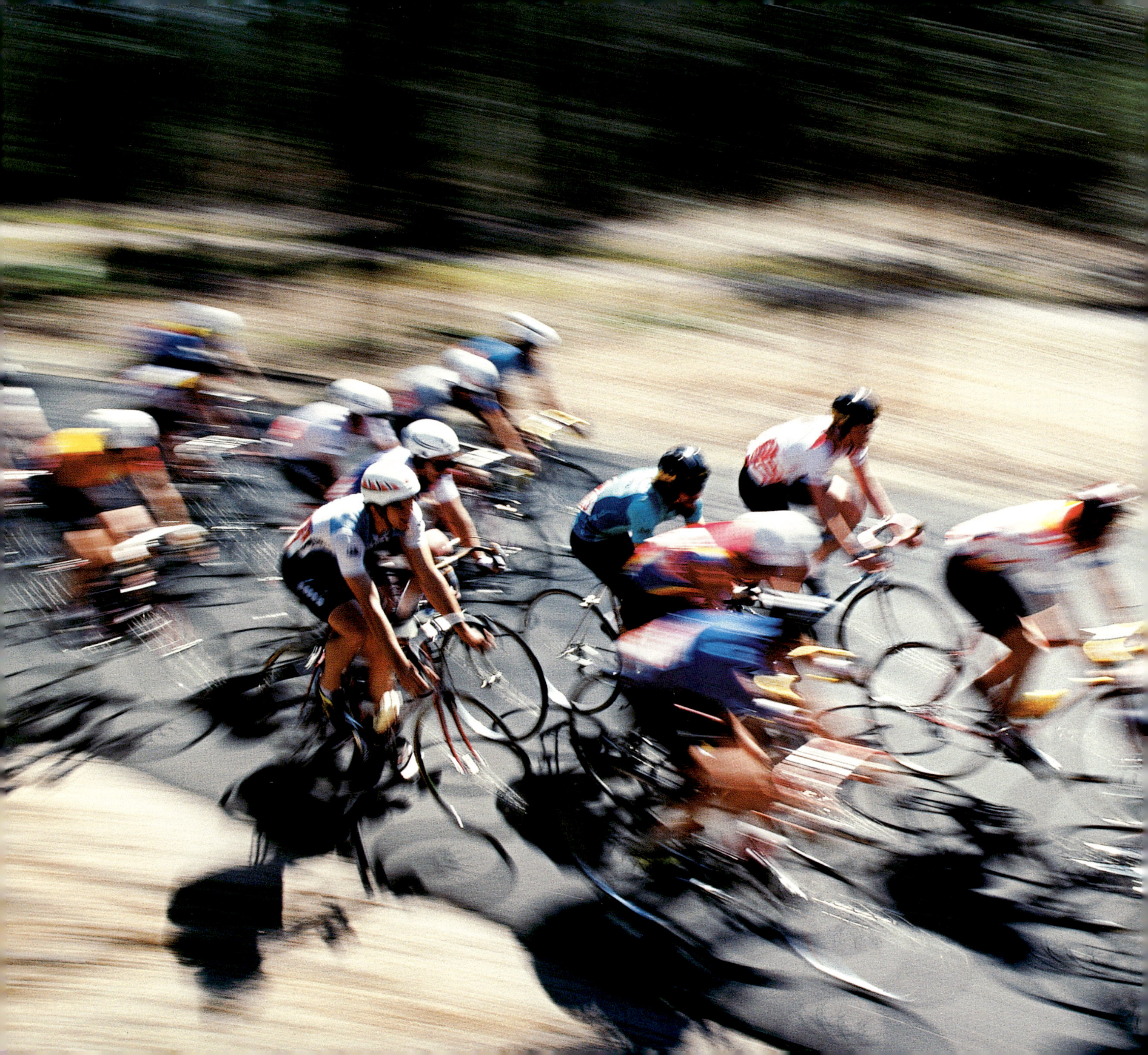

Facing page: Cycling in coastal South Carolina is an increasingly popular sport. These cyclists are competing in a race at Hilton Head High School. Eric Horan

Below: The world seems to slow down at the serene Palmetto Bay Marina in Hilton Head. Eric Horan

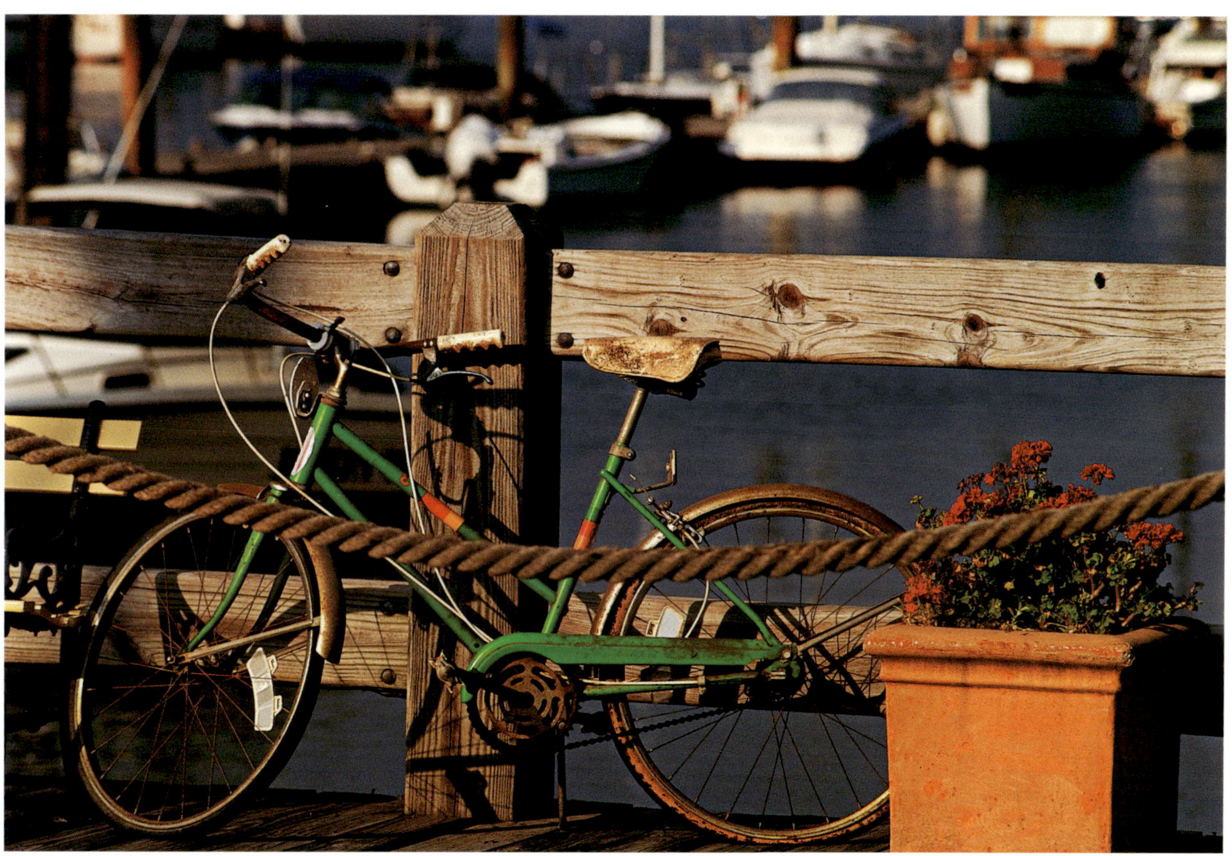

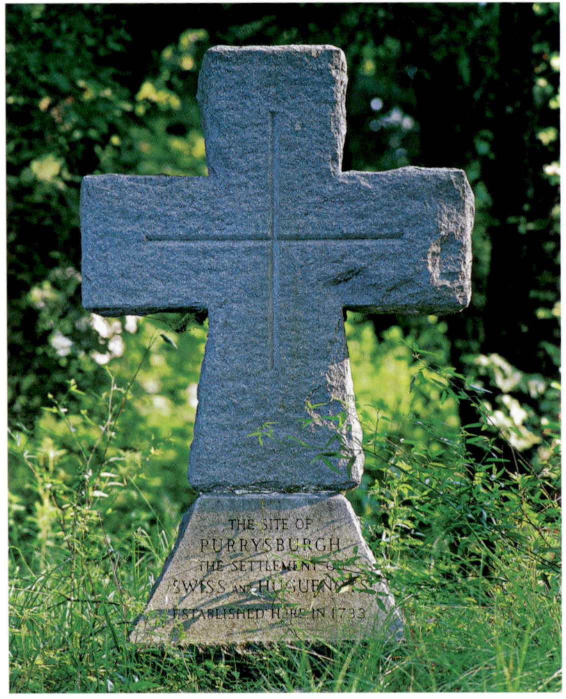

Above: The pre-Revolutionary village of Purrysburgh was settled in 1732 by Swiss-German immigrants who quickly found the insect-infested, swampy land inhospitable. Today, a cross-shaped monument on the banks of the Savannah River marks the site of the abandoned settlement. Eric Horan

Right: Raven Cliff Falls, a 420-foot cascade that delights trekkers at the end of a moderately strenuous two-mile trail, is just one of the attractions of the Mountain Bridge Wilderness Area in northwestern South Carolina. Ron Anderson

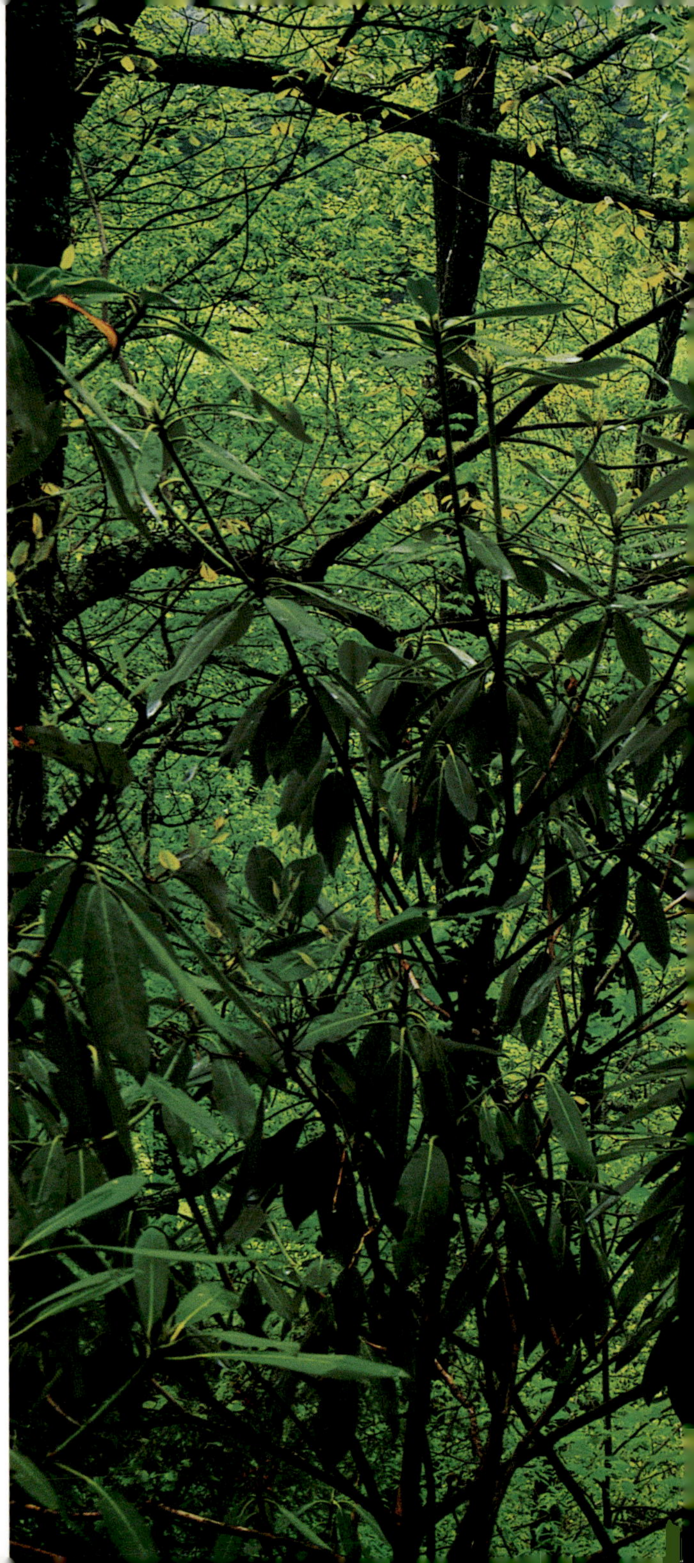

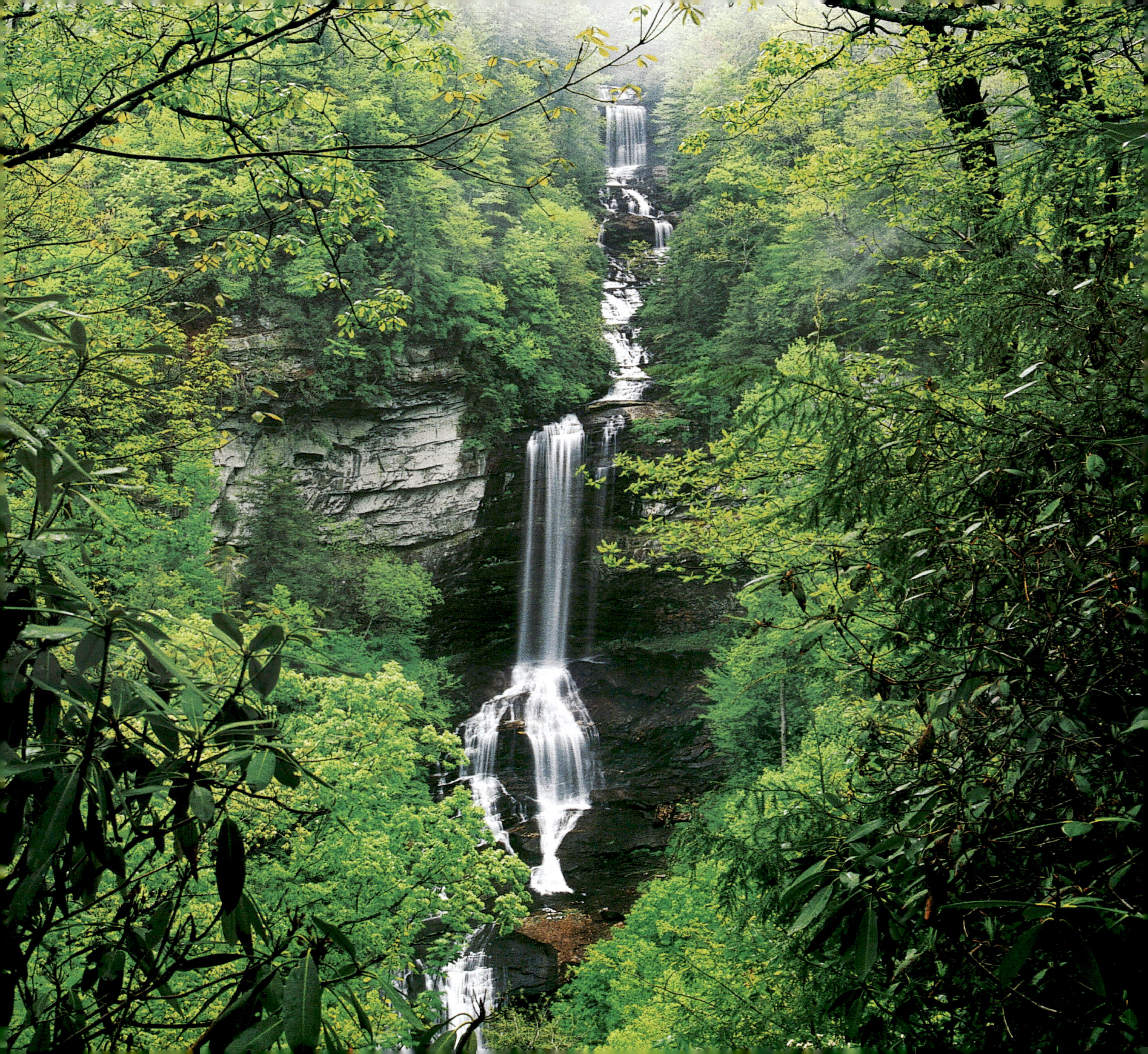

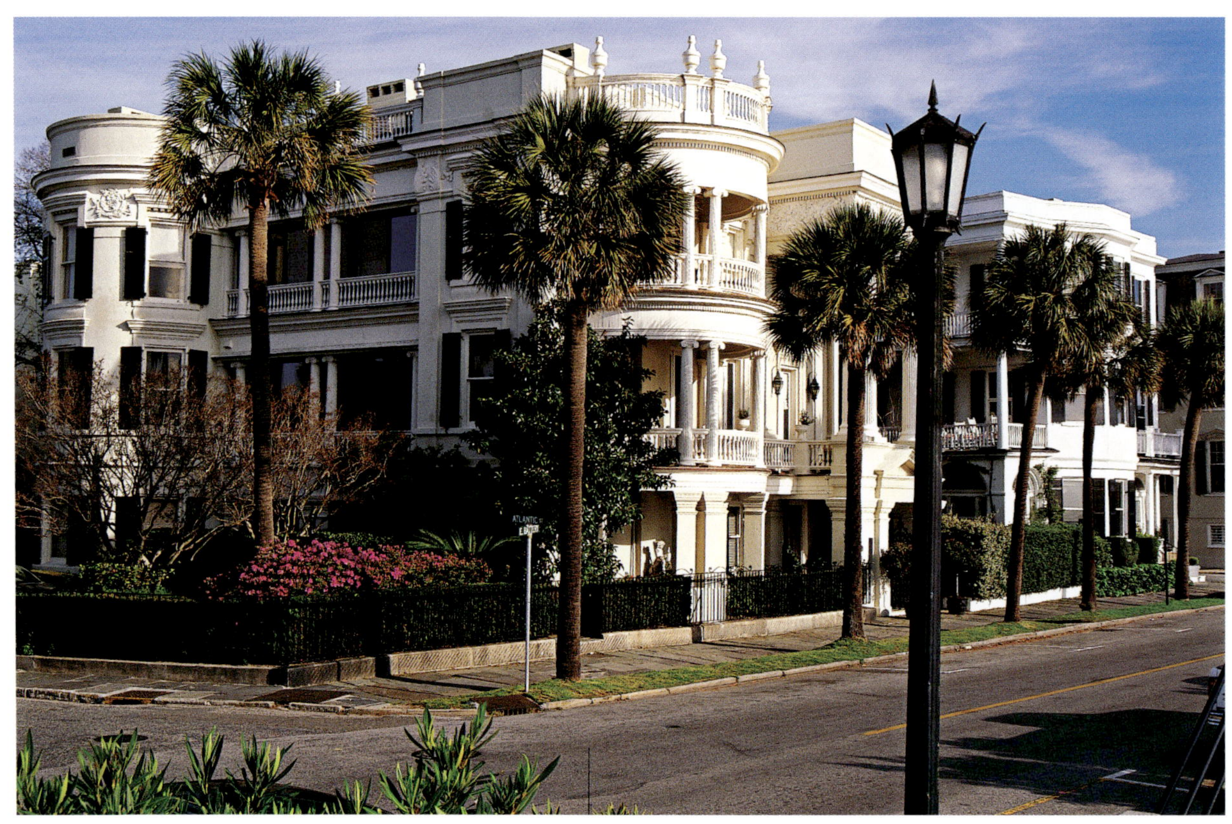

Elegant, palatial homes distinguish the Battery area of downtown Charleston. In April 1861, residents of these homes were witness to the beginning of the Civil War as secessionists fired on Union-held Fort Sumter. The Northern troops were forced to evacuate the fort the next day. Ron Anderson

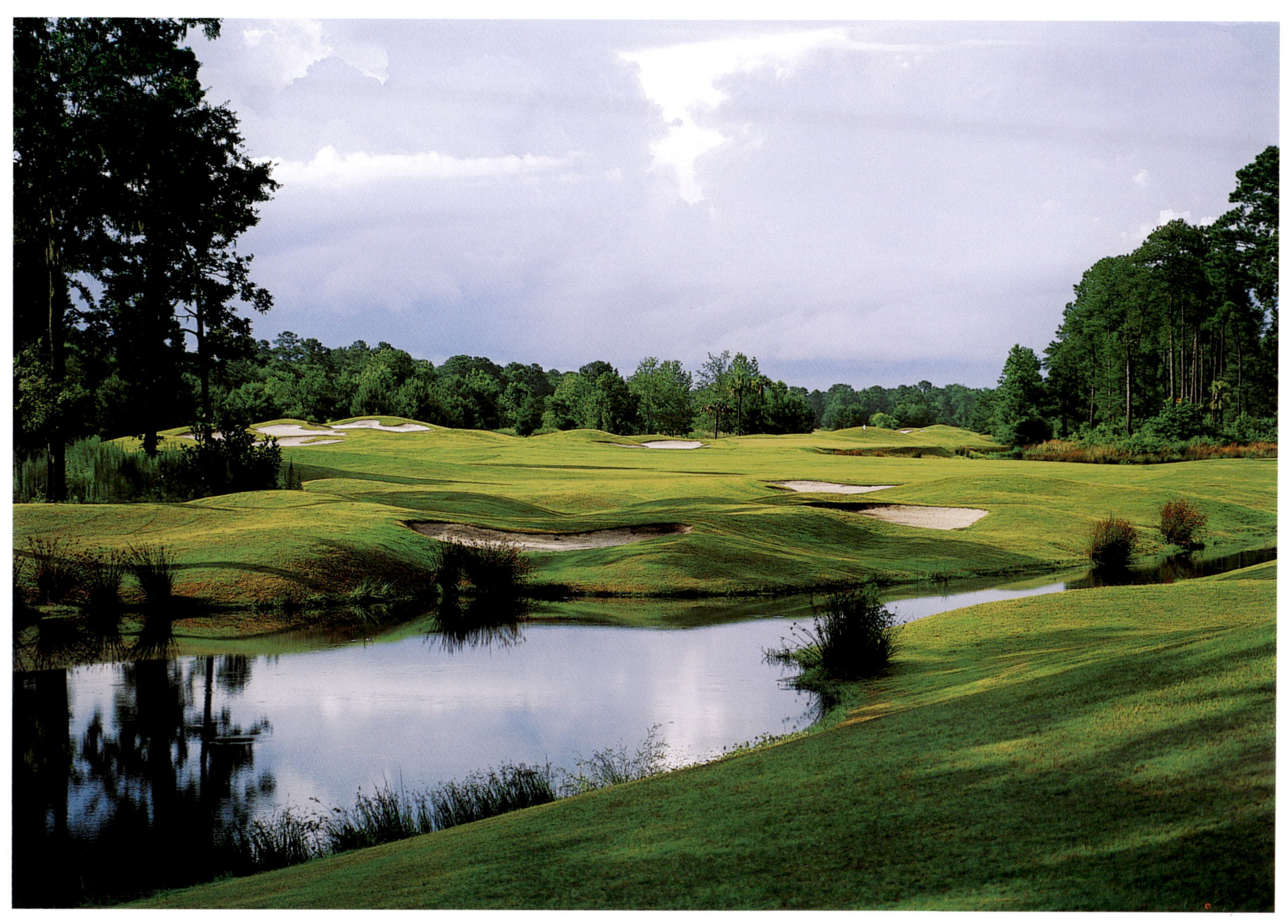

Old Tabby Links at Spring Island, one of Arnold Palmer's finest designs, attracts golfers seeking its picturesque fairways and lush greens. Eric Horan

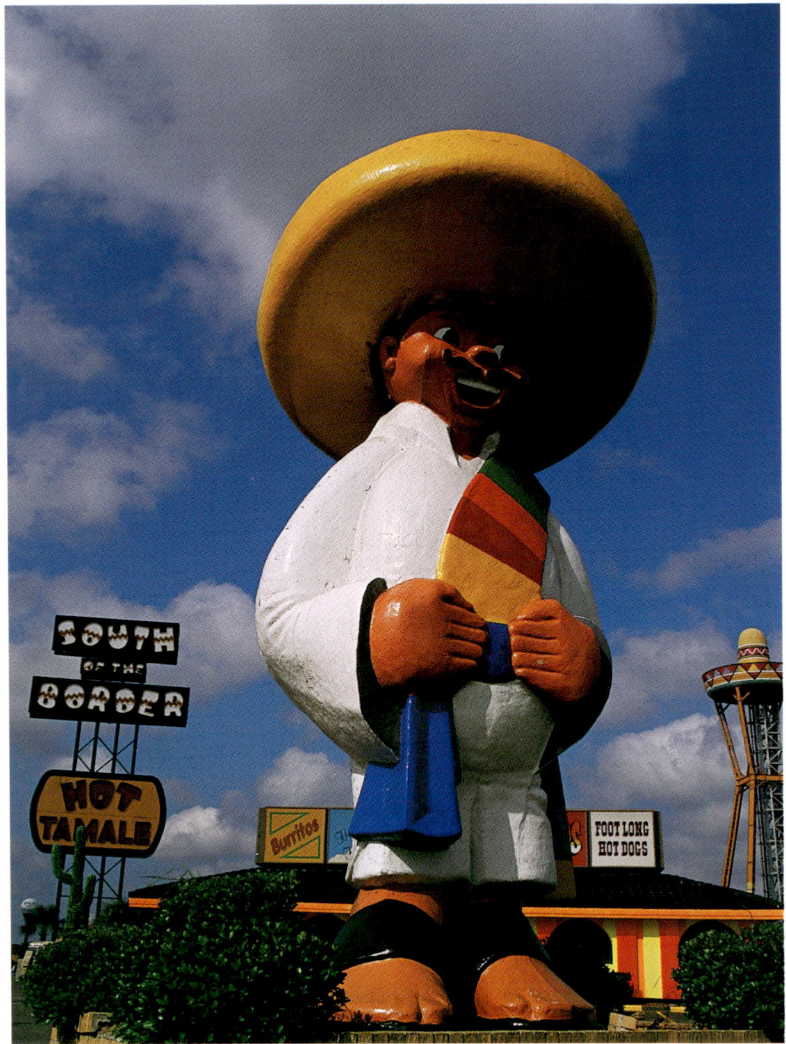

Above: For a taste of roadside Americana, be sure to visit Pedro's South of the Border on Interstate 95, recognizable by its 200-foot-tall sombrero tower (background). Eric Horan

Right: Built in 1981 to serve as a symbol of one of South Carolina's most delectable and prolific crops, the "Peachoid" water tank in Gaffney holds an impressive one million gallons to be used by local residents. Ron Anderson

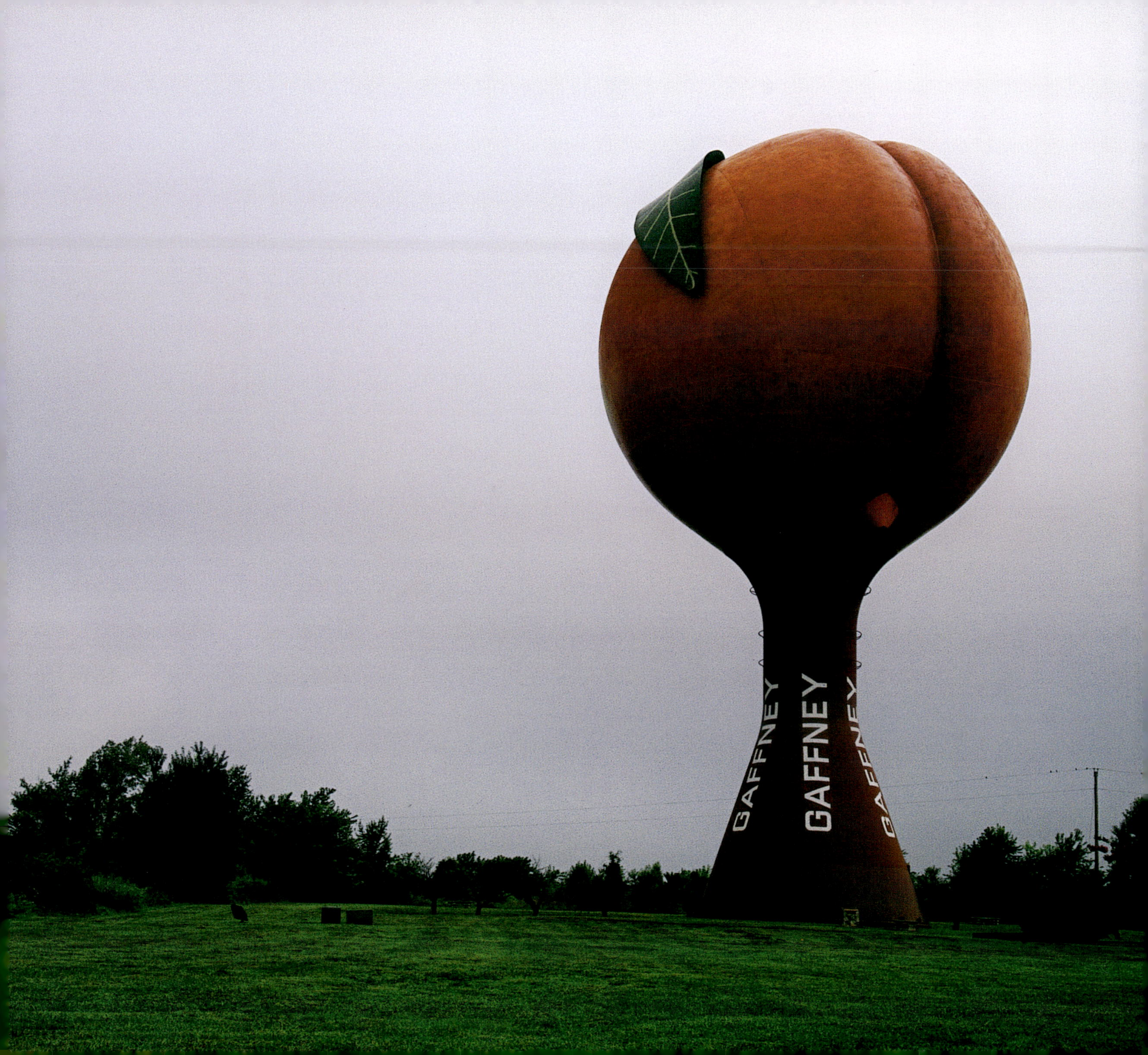
GAFFNEY
GAFFNEY
GAFFNEY

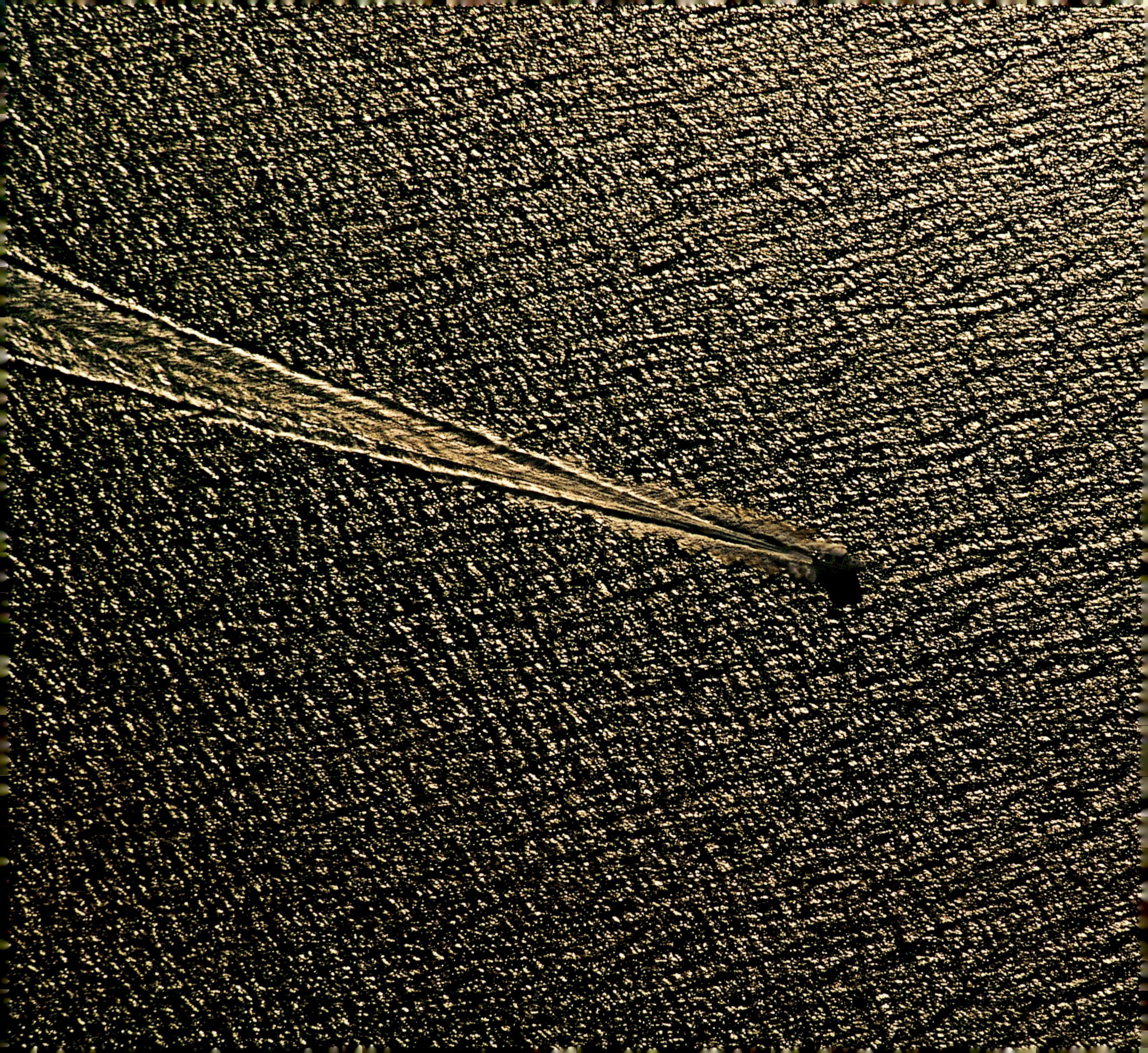

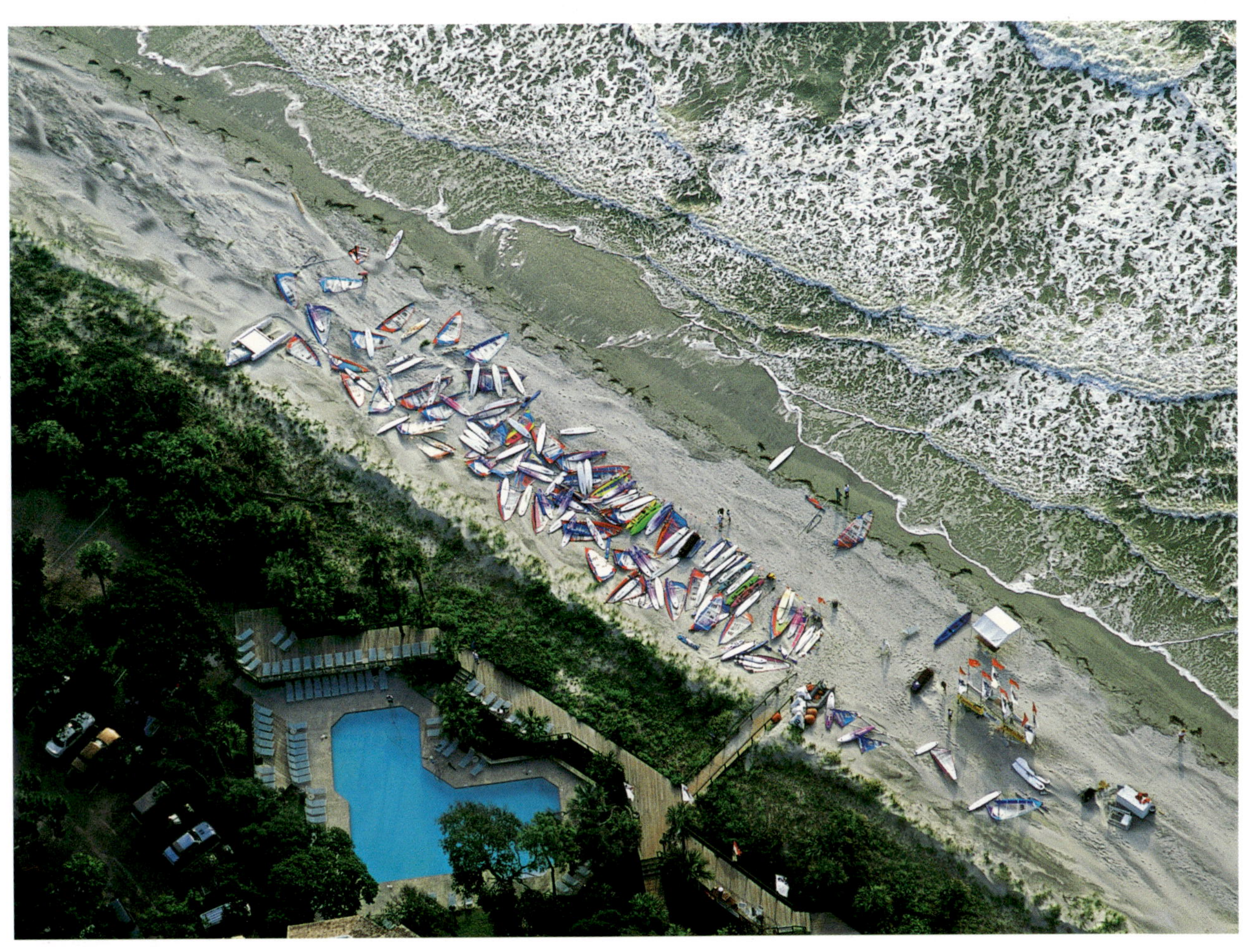

Above: Known for its gracious resort accommodations, its unparalleled recreational opportunities, and its fine coastal charm, Hilton Head is popular with both vacationers and permanent residents. ERIC HORAN

Left: A boat slices through calm waters on the South Carolina coast. ERIC HORAN

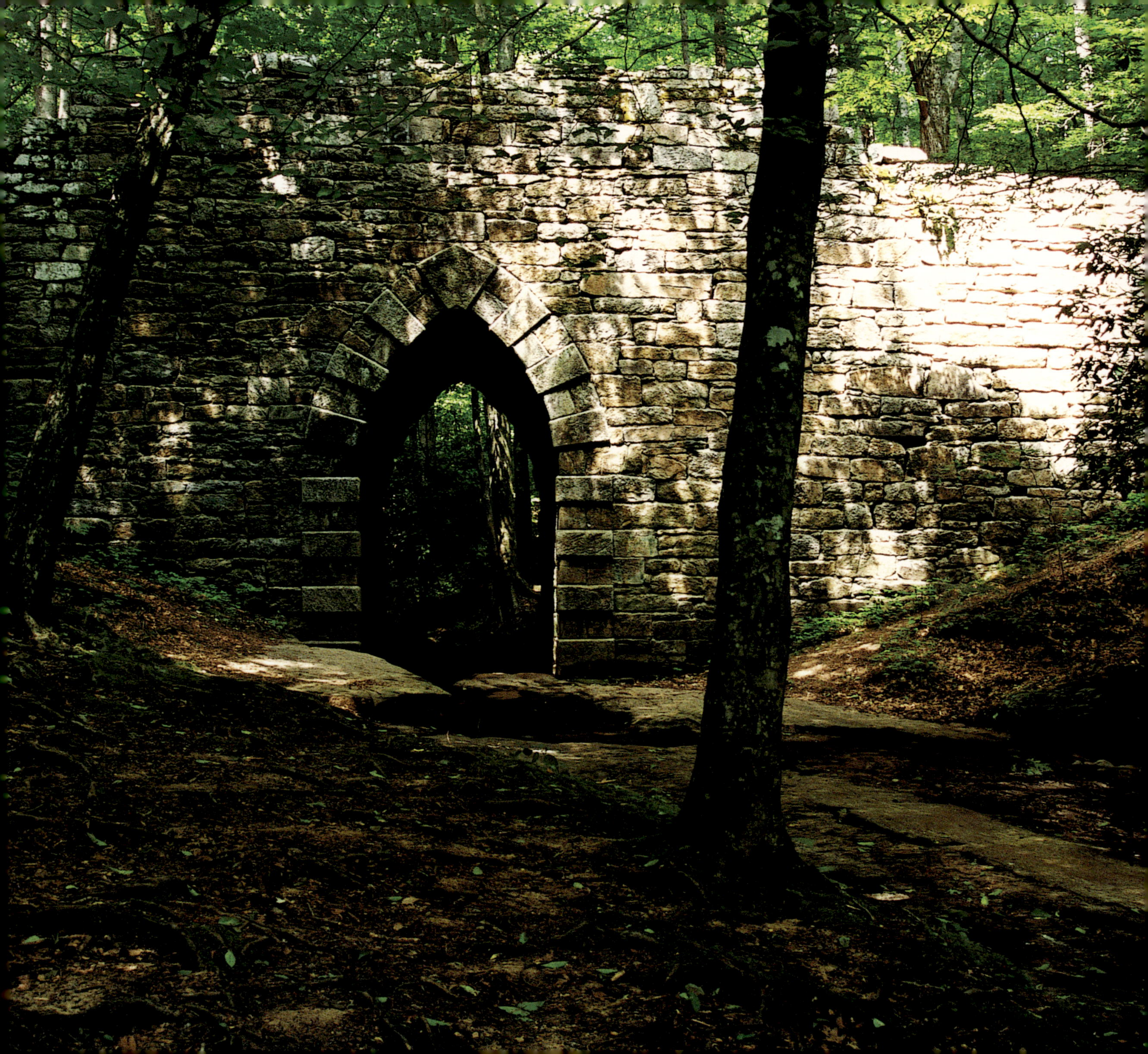

Facing page: The Poinsett Bridge in northern Greenville County was once part of a state road connecting Charleston to the Blue Ridge Mountains. Built in 1820, the structure features an unusual 14-foot Gothic arch and claims the title of the state's oldest bridge. RON ANDERSON

Below: Hikers who follow Reedy Cove Creek in Pickens County will reach impressive Twin Falls, two waterfalls that cascade over rocky ledges. The taller of the pair drops a dramatic 75 feet. RON ANDERSON

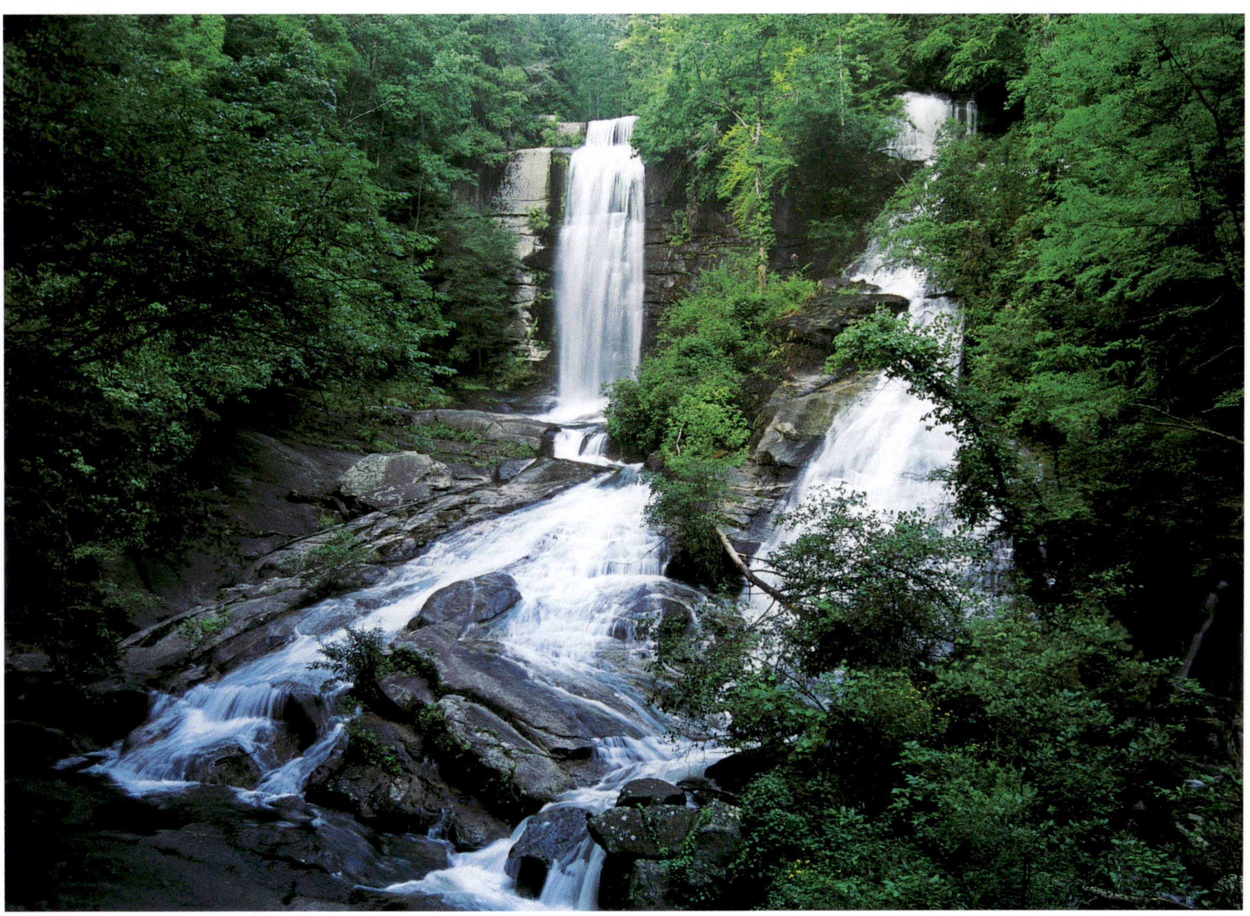

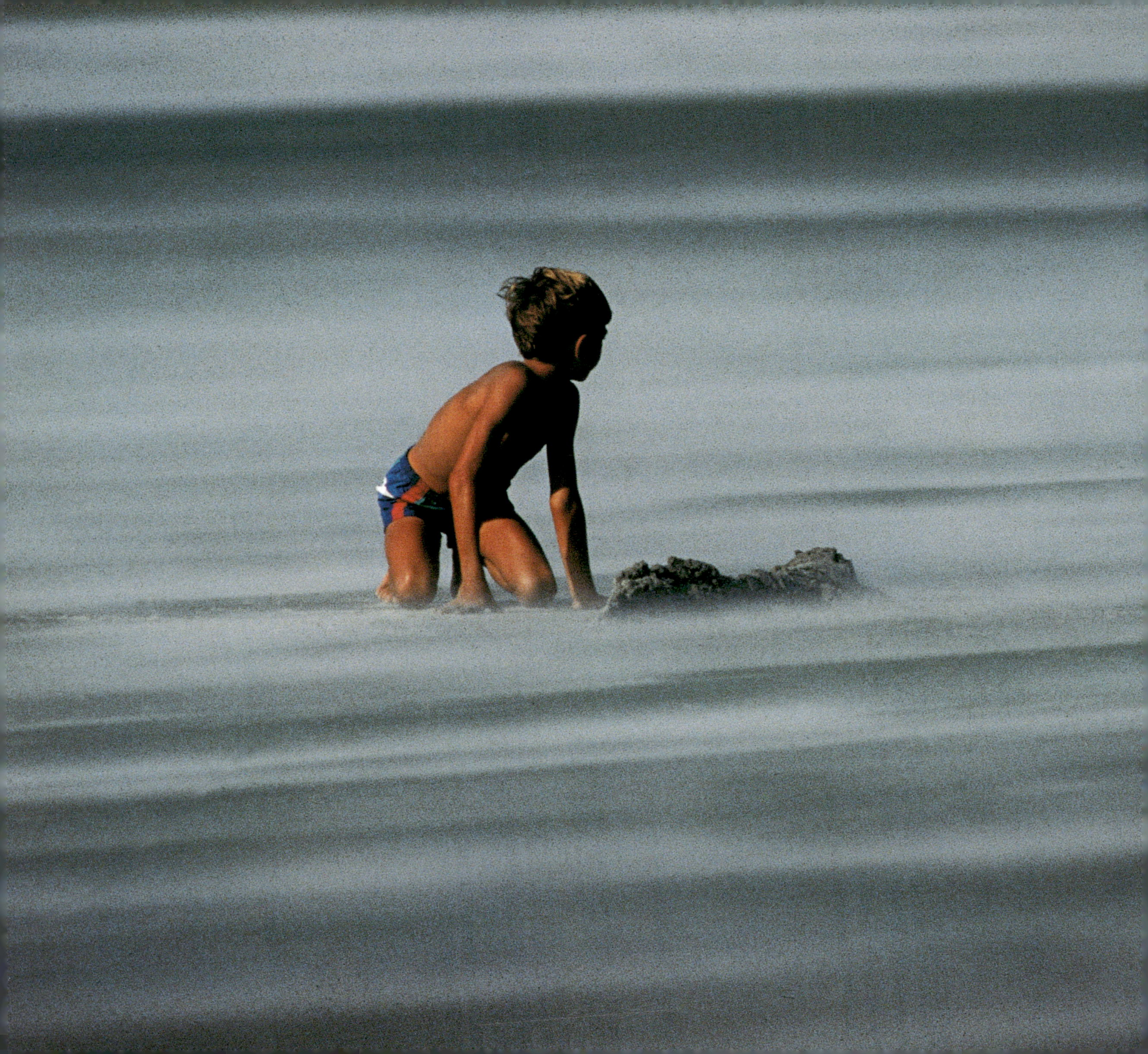

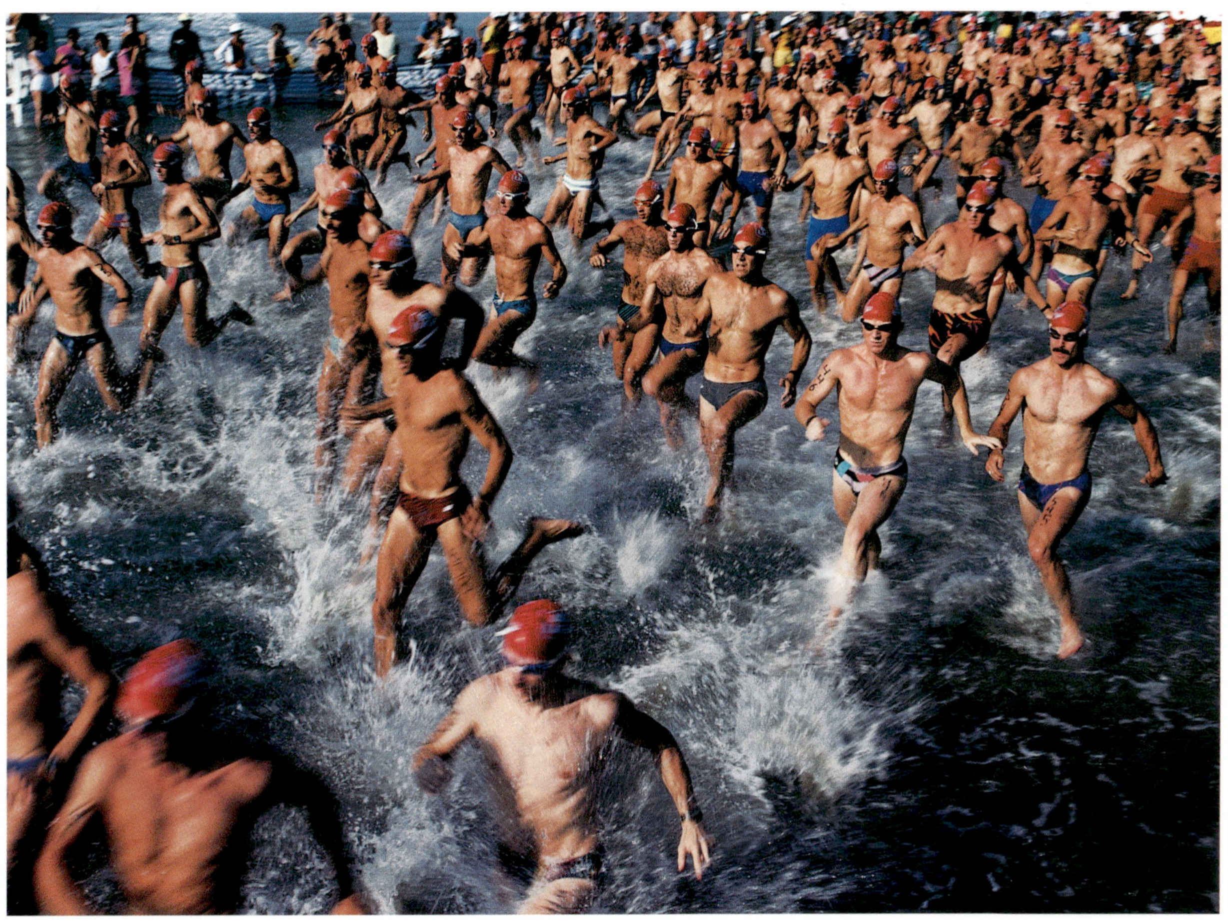

Above: Triathletes embark on the swimming portion of the competition. South Carolina hosts several triathlons each year. ERIC HORAN

Left: A youngster at Sea Pines Beach braves blowing sand to continue fortifying his sand castle. ERIC HORAN

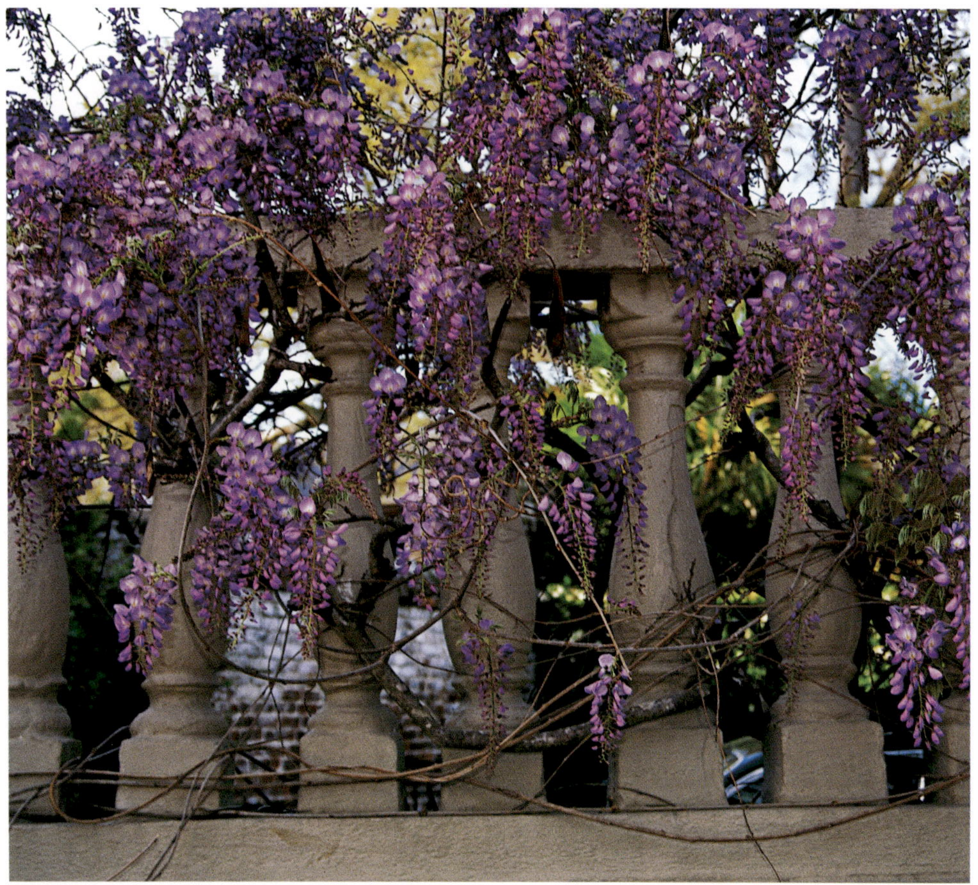

Above: Many Southerners would agree that spring is the state's loveliest season, with the azaleas, dogwoods, wisteria, and other plants in full bloom. Here clusters of purple wisteria drape an elegant Charleston garden. RON ANDERSON

Right: Expansive grounds provide an inviting setting for Grove Plantation, an 1828 home near Adams Run that is one of only three Ashepoo, Combahee, and Edisto (ACE) Basin plantations to survive the Civil War. Renovated in 1964 and 1996-97, today it serves as the headquarters for the U.S. Fish and Wildlife Service's ACE Basin National Wildlife Refuge and the Nature Conservancy's ACE Basin Bioreserve Office. ERIC HORAN

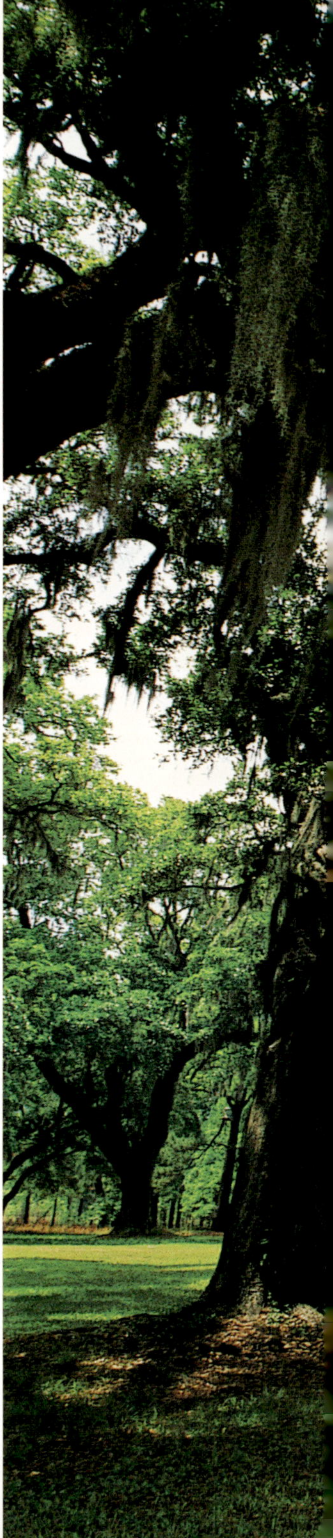

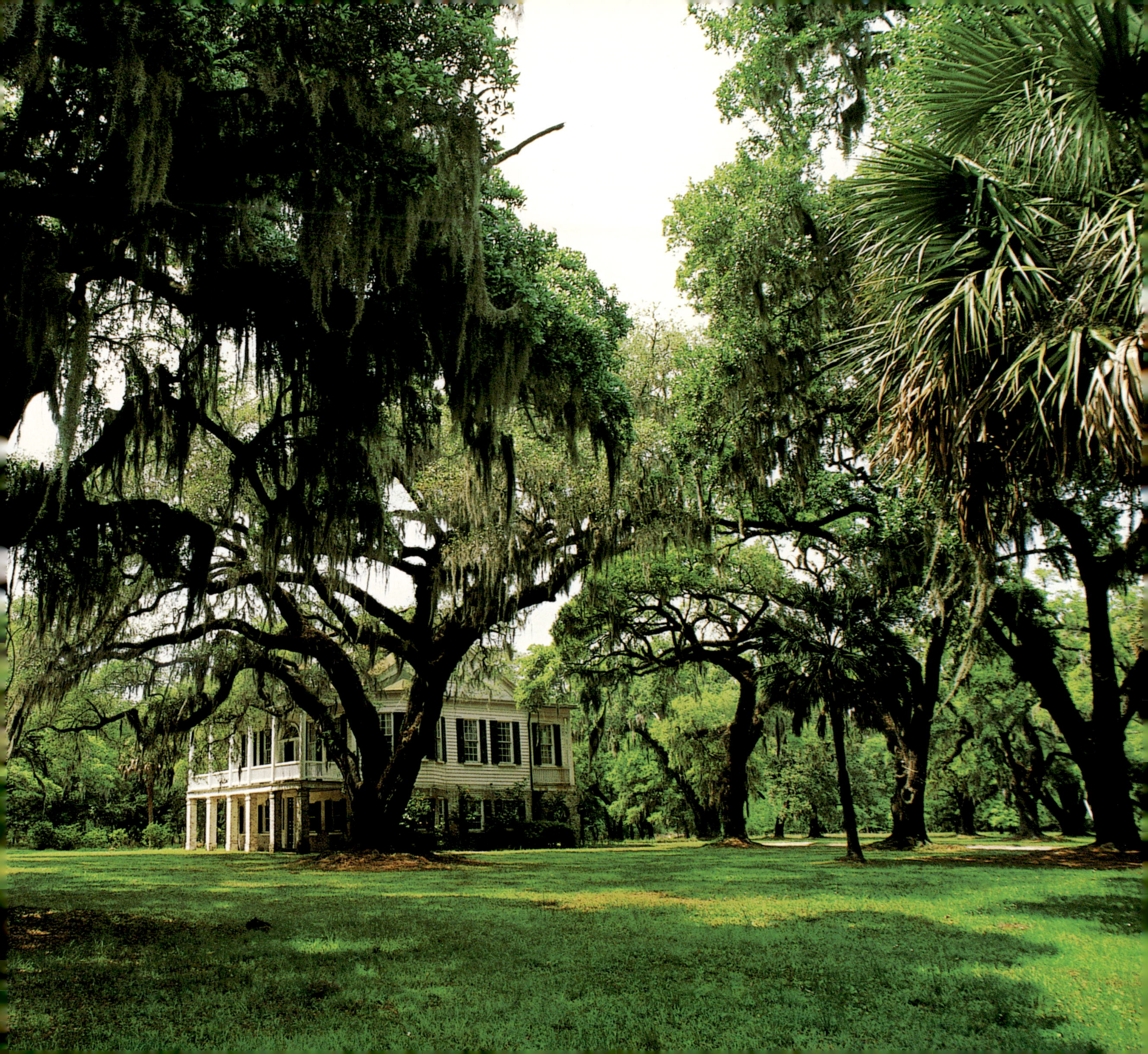

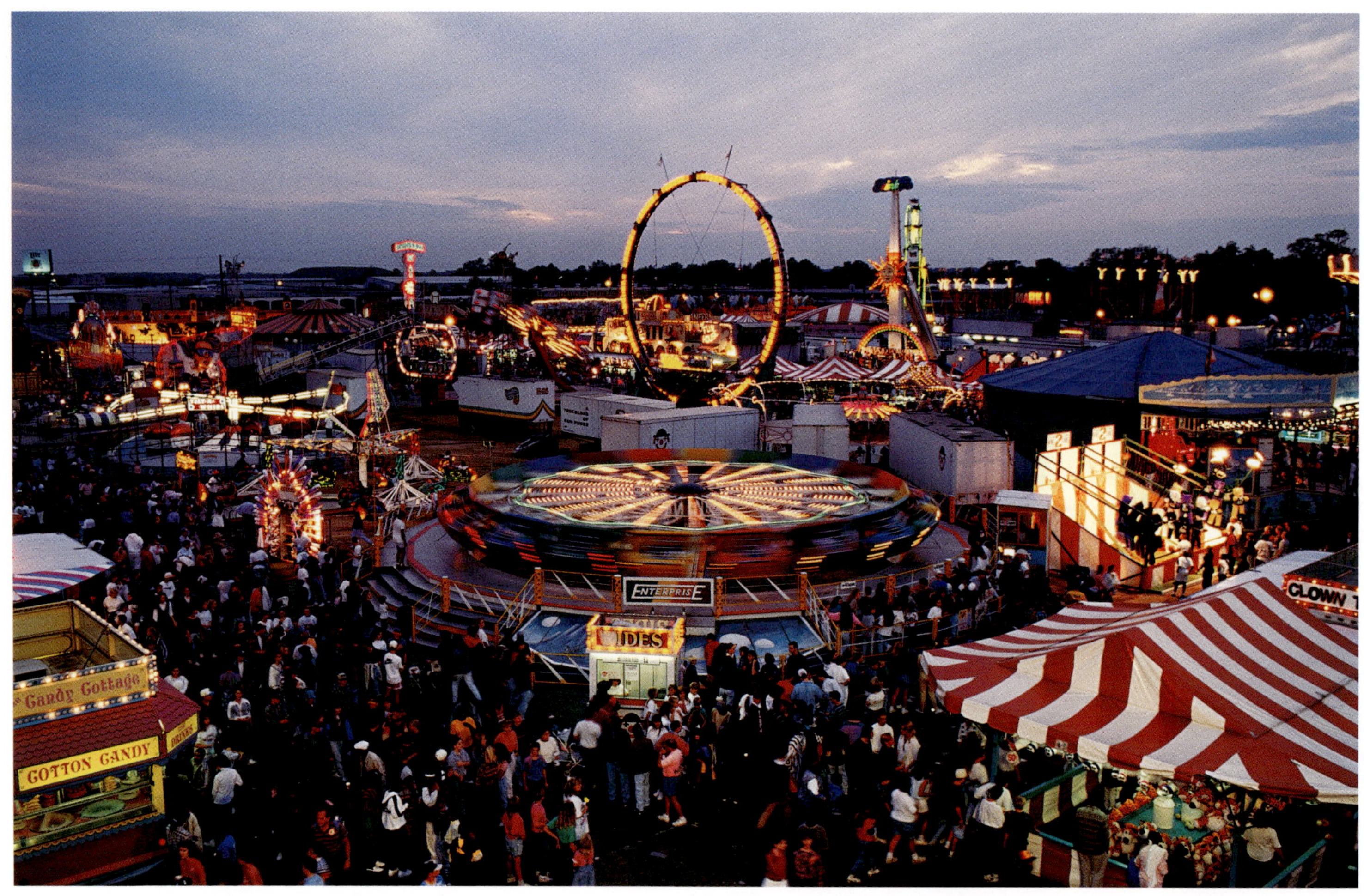

Above: October would not be complete without a visit to the annual State Fair held in Columbia. Award-winning artwork and photography, live evening entertainment, and fiercely contested livestock judgings complement the wide range of heart-stopping rides. Eric Horan

Facing page: For more than 50 years, the Myrtle Beach Pavilion Amusement Park has entertained young and old alike with thrilling rides and a variety of interesting performances. Eric Horan

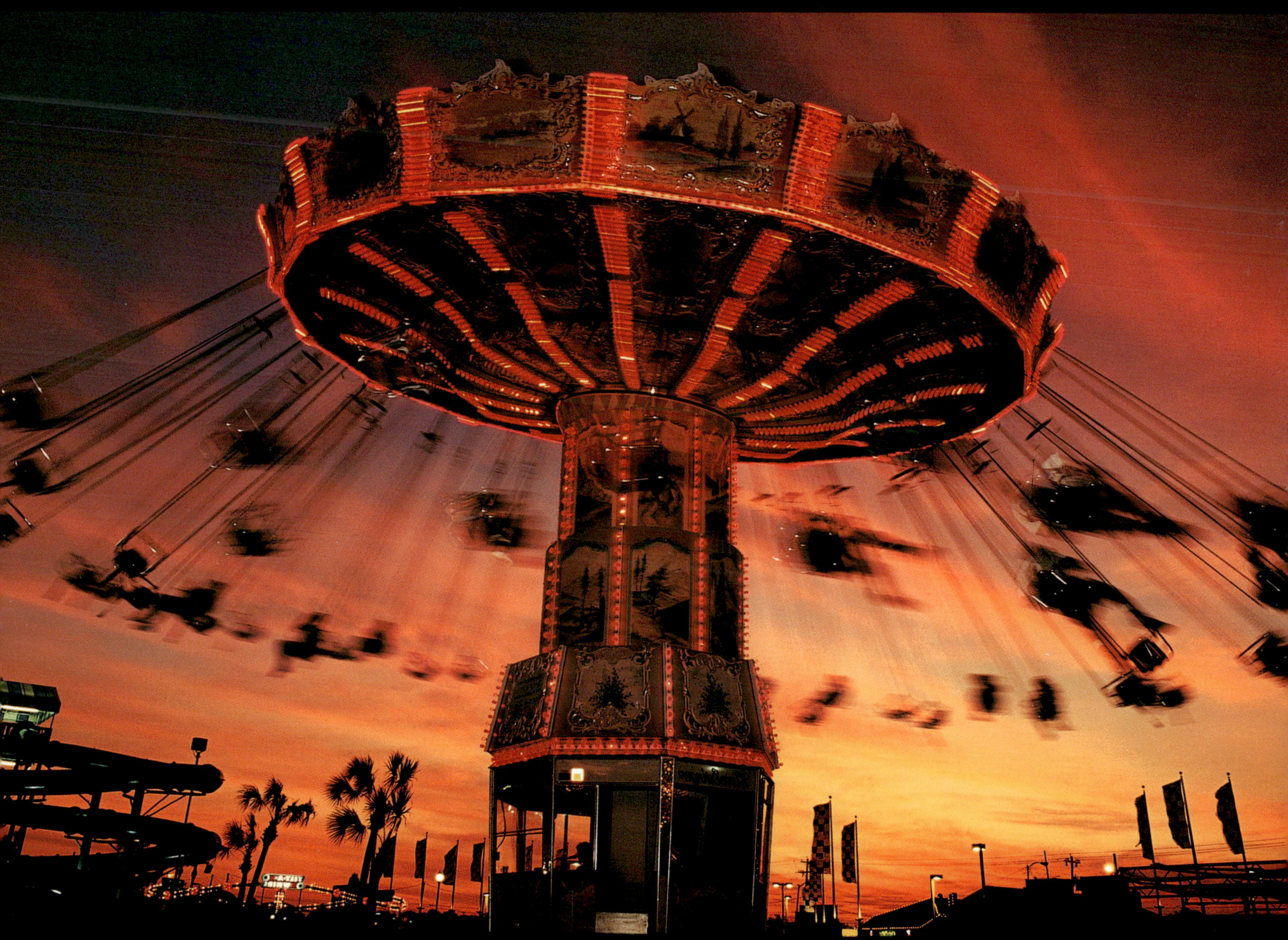

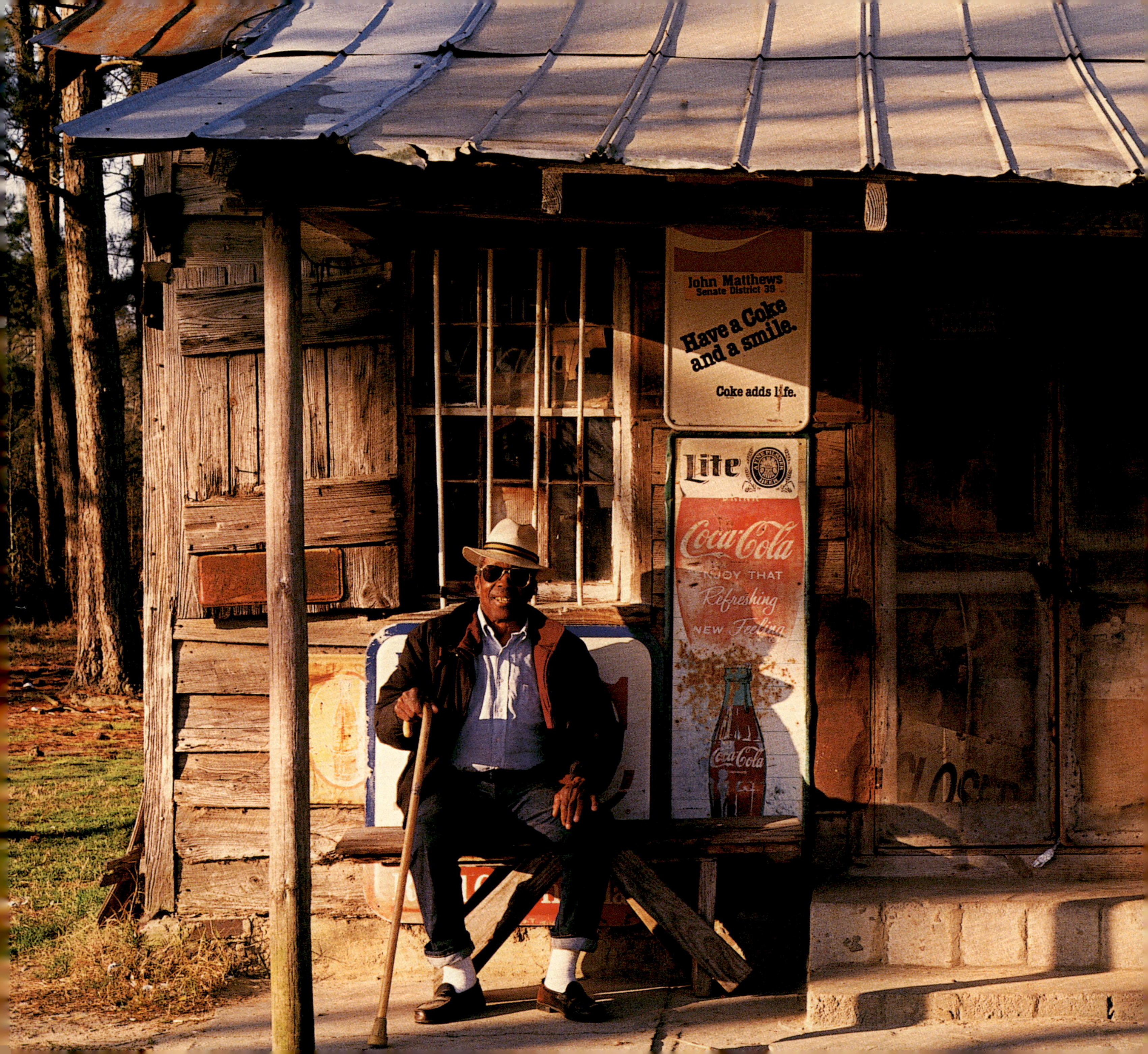
John Matthews
Senate District 39
Have a Coke
and a smile.
Coke adds life.
Lite
Coca-Cola
ENJOY THAT
Refreshing
NEW Feeling

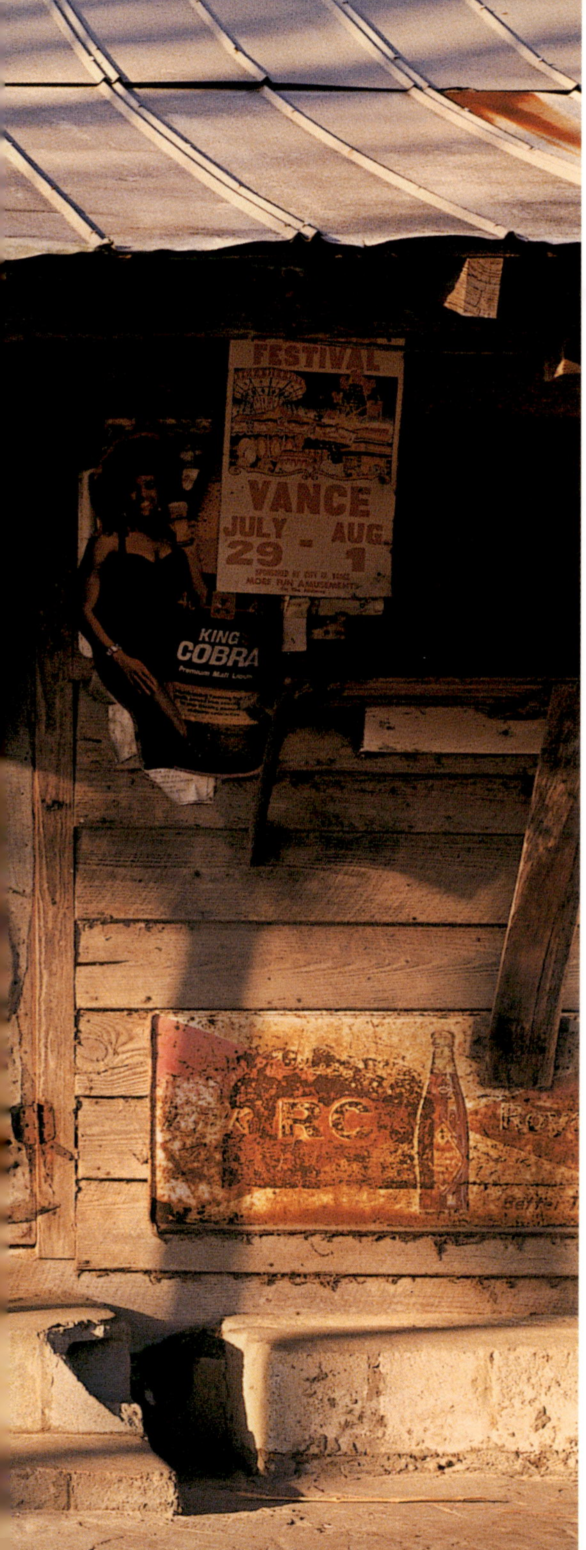

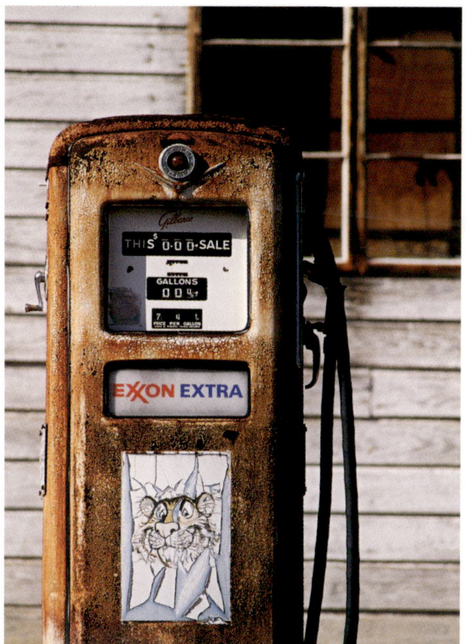

Left: A rusty gas pump guards a backroad filling station on Highway 321.
ERIC HORAN

Far left: An old country store in rural Vance encourages nearby residents to sit on its benches and recall simpler times. ERIC HORAN

Below: An old Pontiac succumbs to the elements.
ERIC HORAN

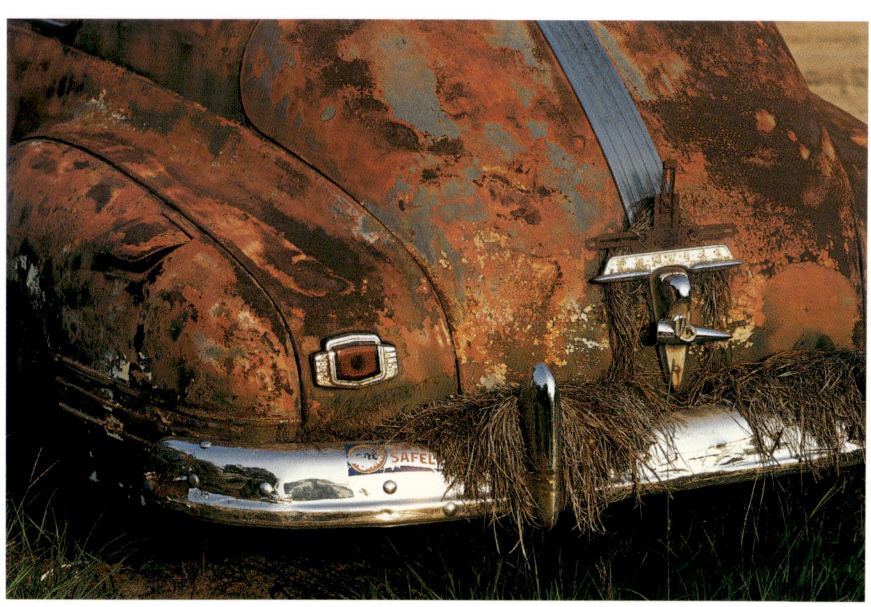

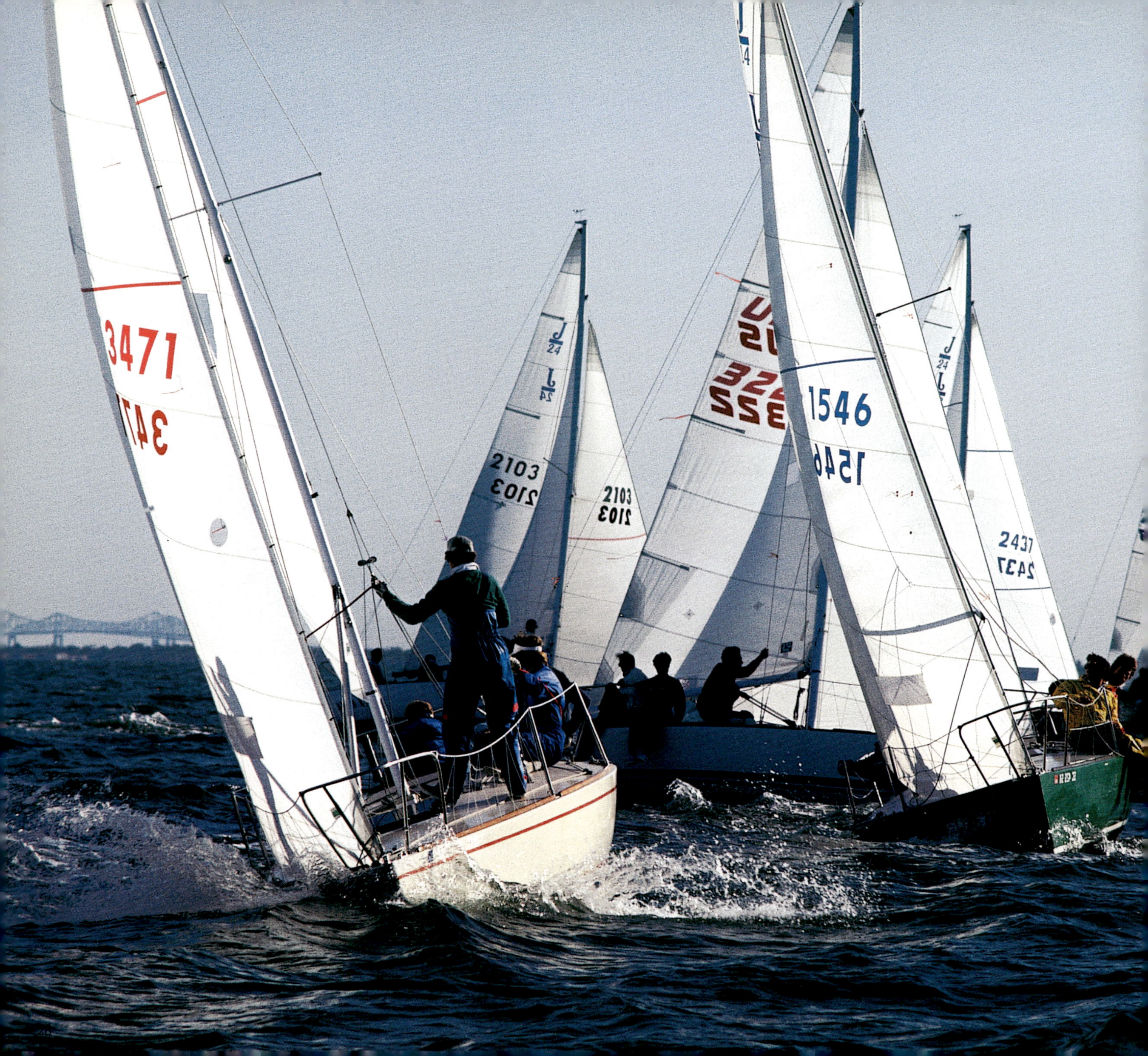
3471
2103
2103
1546
2437

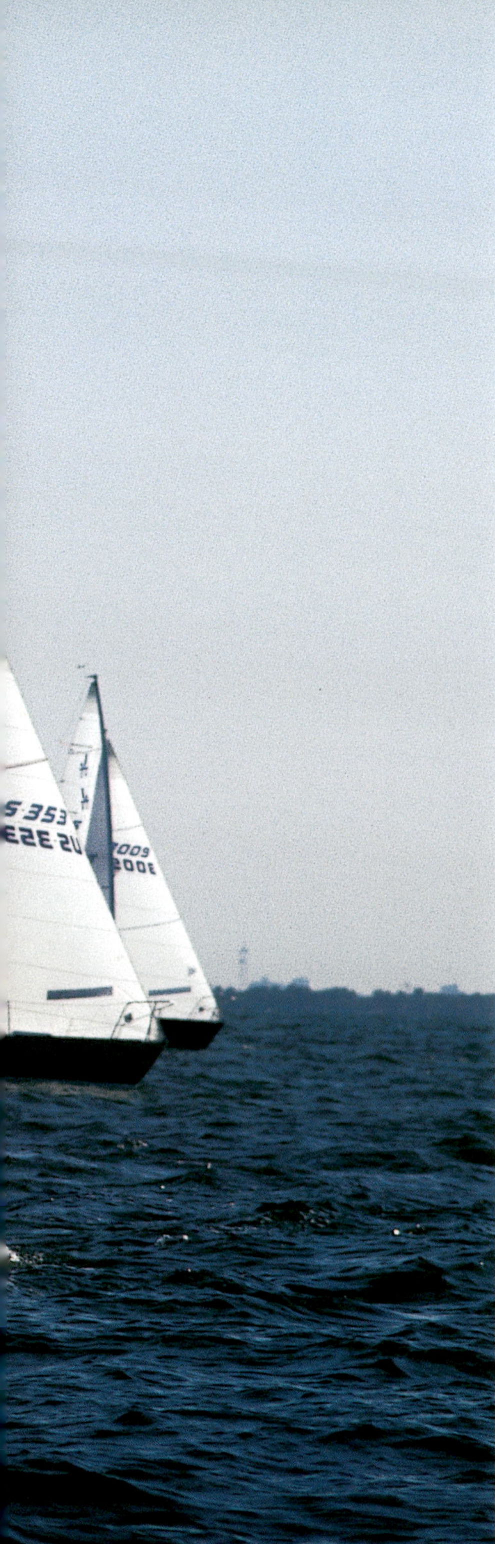

Left: Boats slice through the water in a race hosted by the Charleston Yacht Club. Eric Horan

Below: Kayakers enjoy the intercoastal waterways at Parris Island. Eric Horan

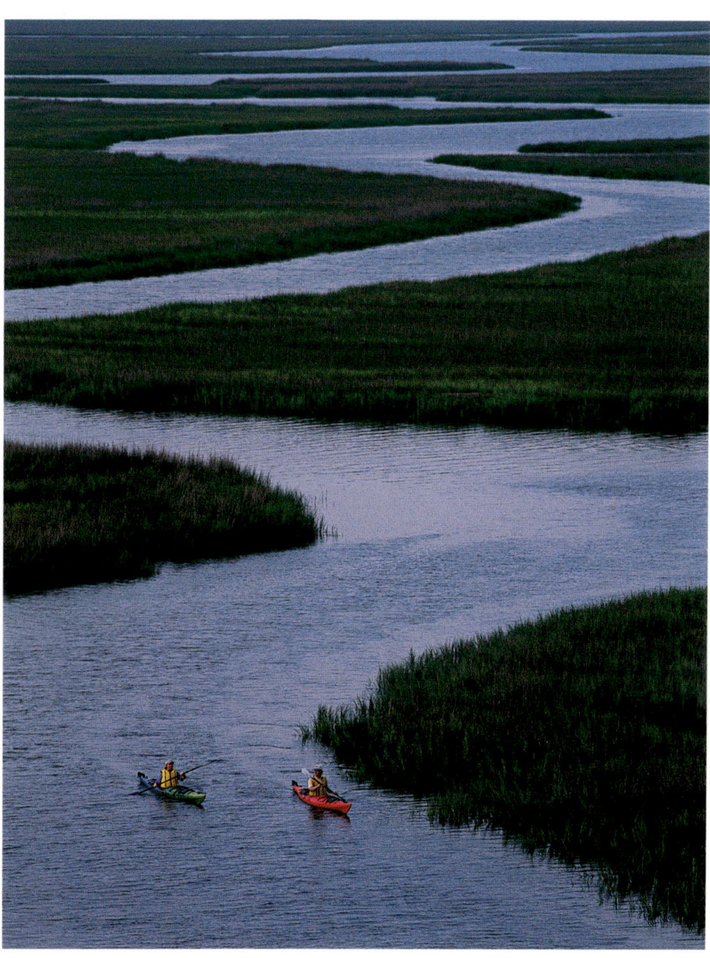

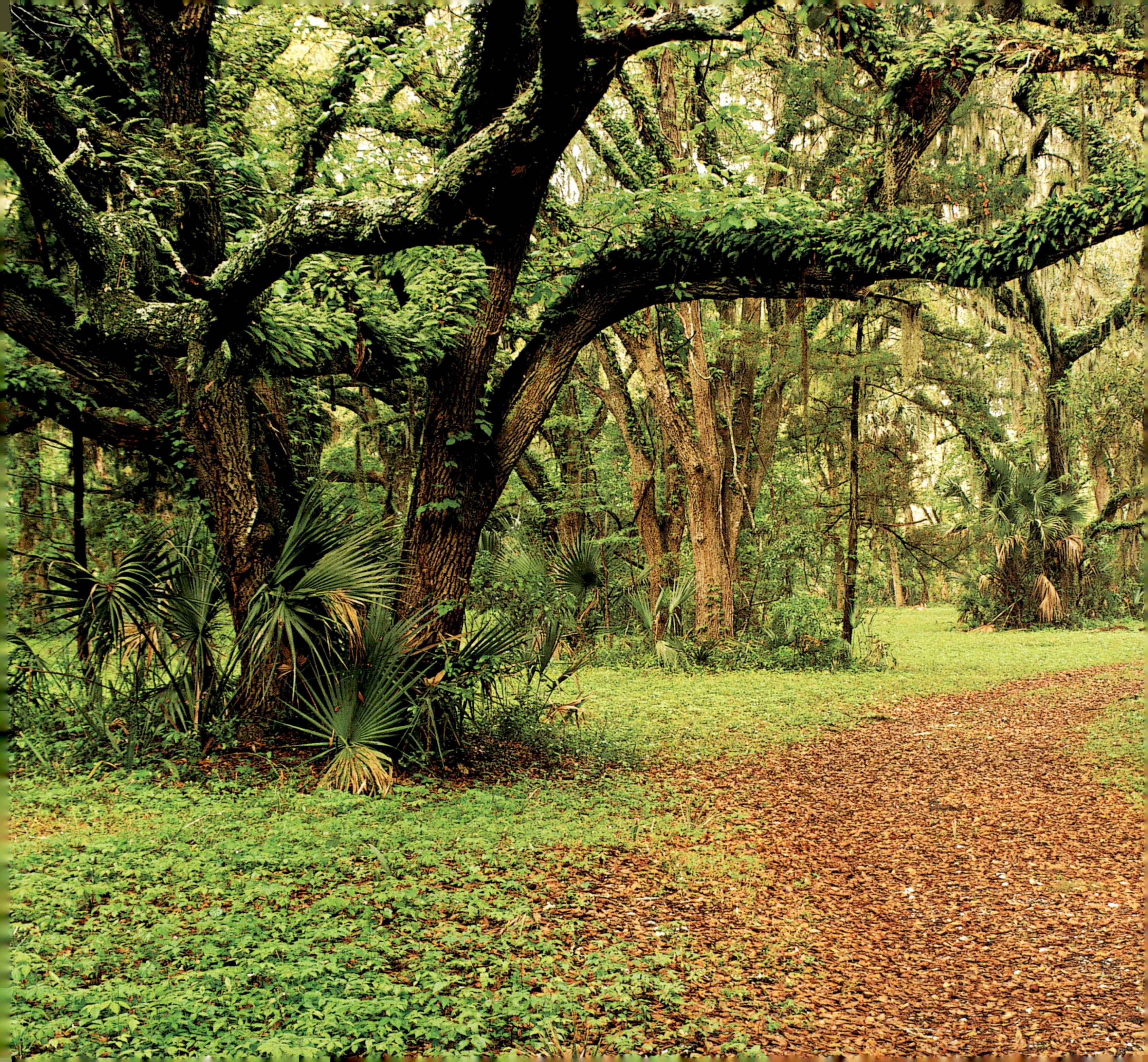

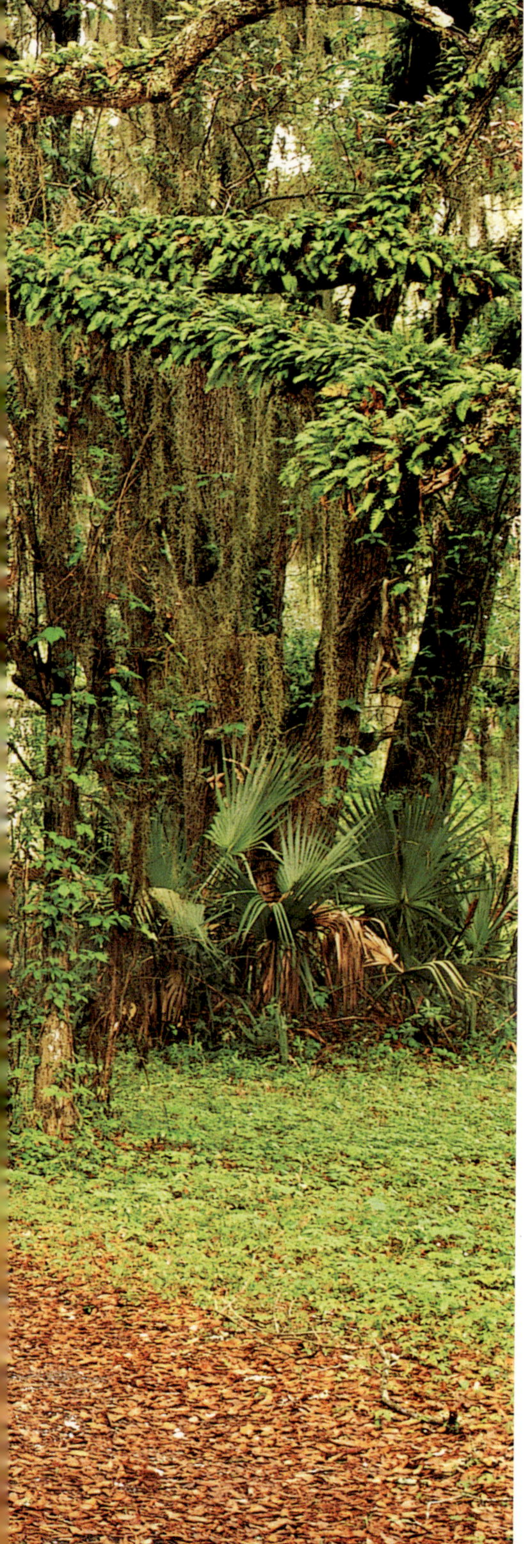

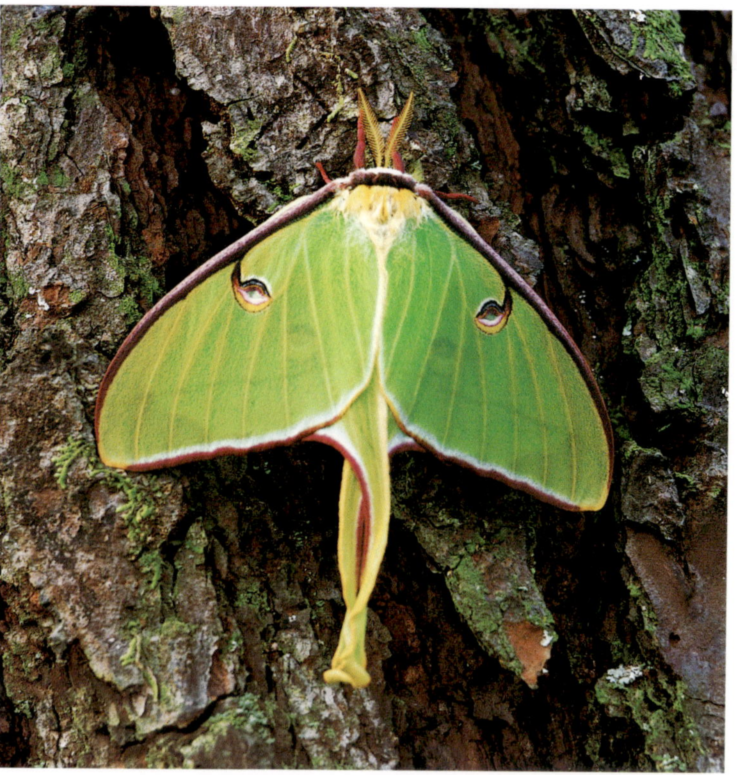

Above: With unique yellow-green coloration and a wingspan of four and a half inches, the luna moth is a delight to see. The female lays about 200 eggs on the underside of black walnut leaves and, her duty done, dies shortly thereafter. Ron Anderson

Left: An inviting path winds its way through ancient oak trees draped with Spanish moss at Spring Island in the heart of South Carolina's Lowcountry. Eric Horan

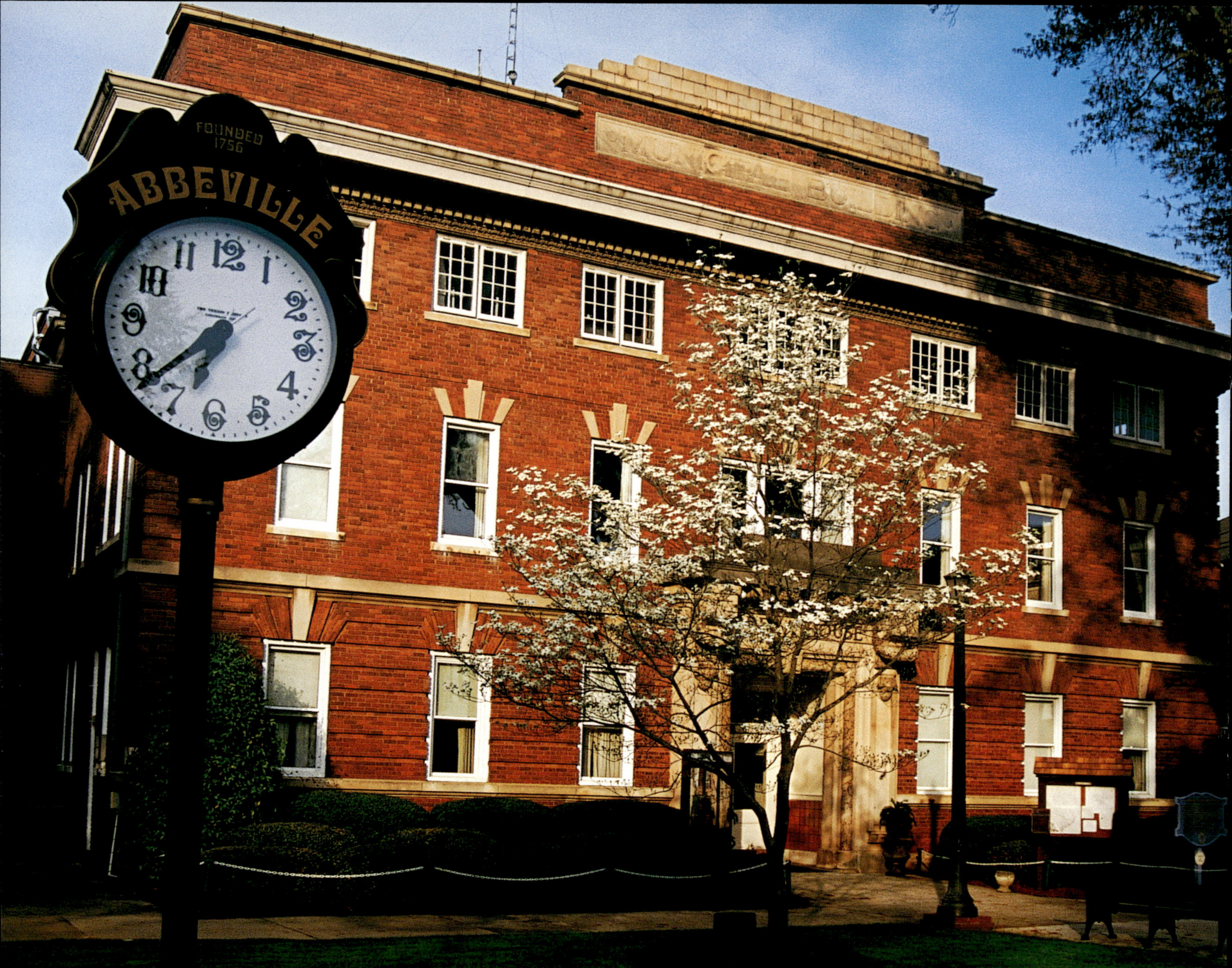
FOUNDED
1756
ABBEVILLE

Left: Western South Carolina's Old 96 District is home to the 1909 Abbeville Opera House, where two theater companies perform. Ron Anderson

Below: Azaleas, the much-loved bloom of South Carolina's spring, flower in the upcountry of Pickens County. Ron Anderson

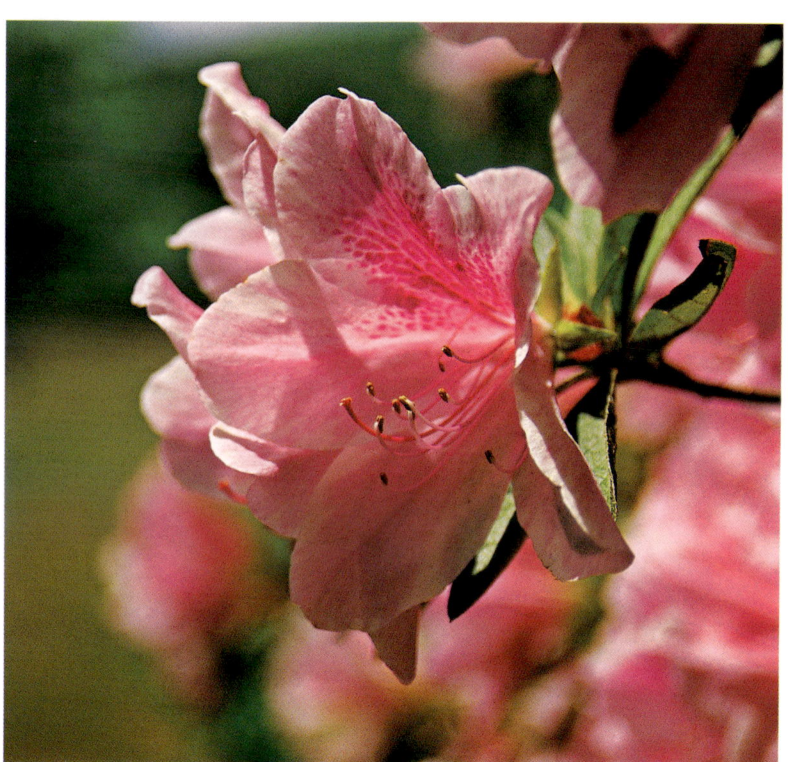

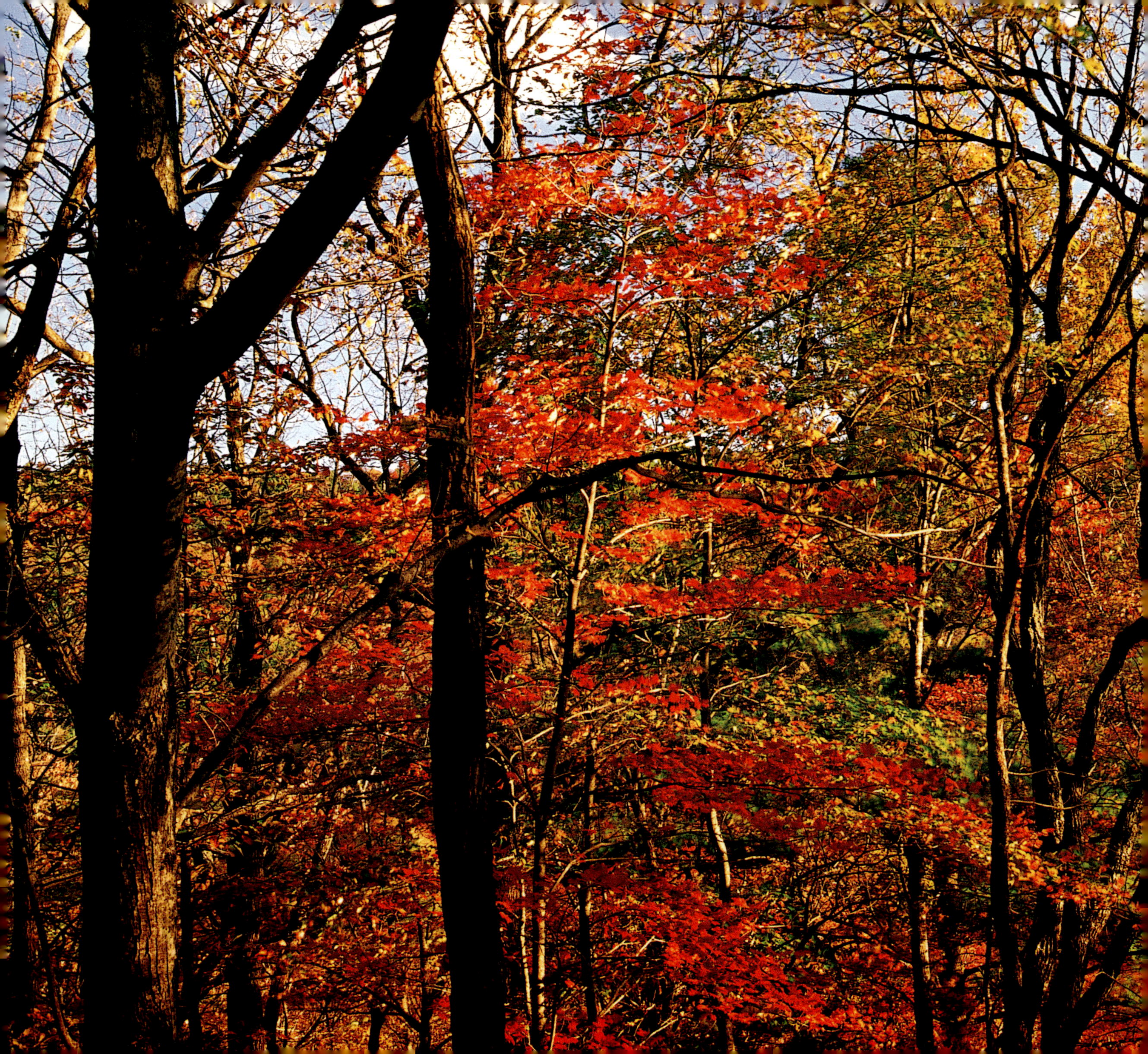

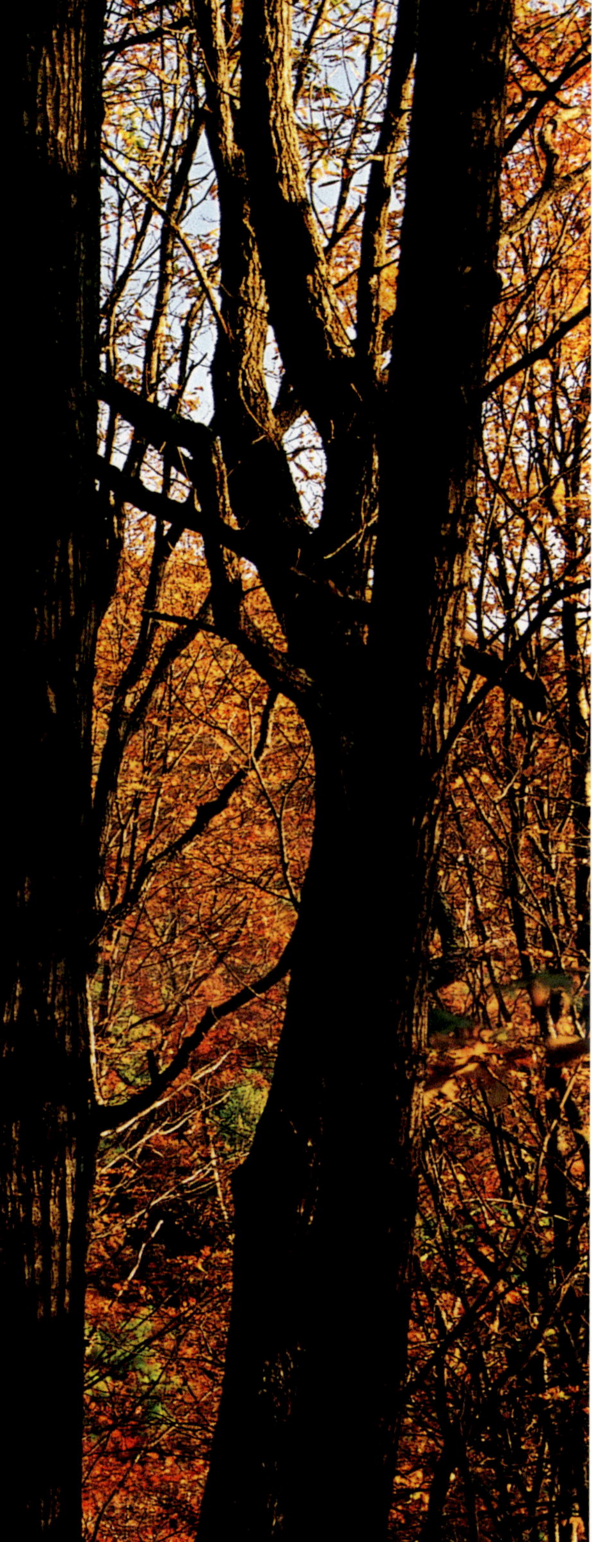

Left: Autumn foliage greets visitors to Sumter National Forest, once home to the Cherokee nation. Today the forest's crown jewel is undoubtedly the Chattooga River, a primary destination for whitewater enthusiasts in the Southeast. Ron Anderson

Below: Edgefield's Wild Turkey Center and Museum, headquarters of the National Wild Turkey Federation, is devoted exclusively to the conservation of the bird Benjamin Franklin wanted as the United States' national emblem instead of the bald eagle. The wild turkey is the state game bird of South Carolina. Ron Anderson

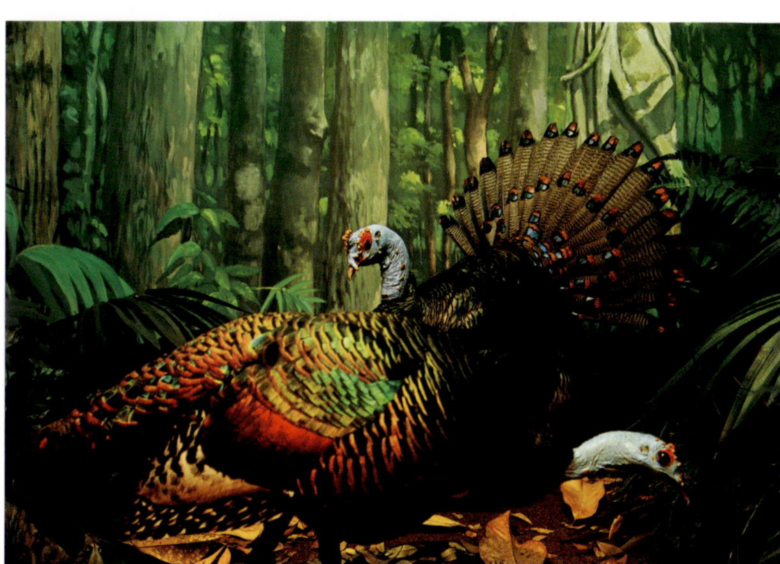

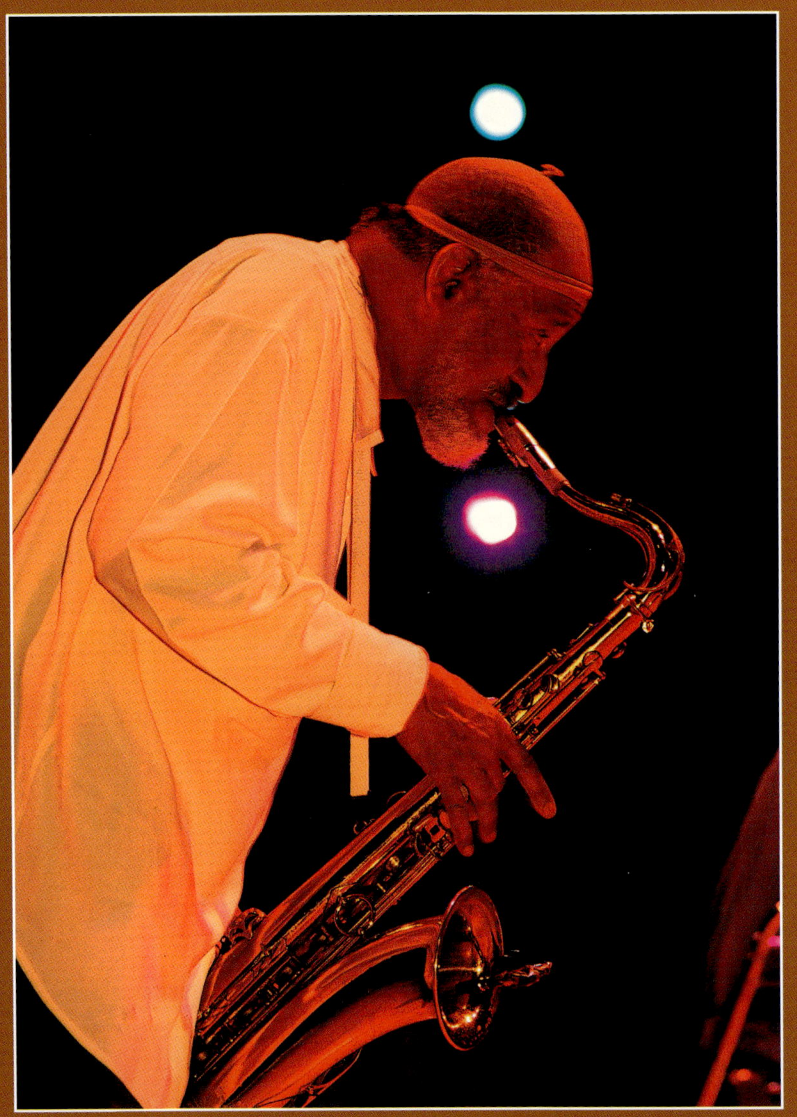

Jazz great Sonny Rollins performs at Charleston's annual Spoleto Festival. The 17-day world-class festival features opera, theater, dance, music, and visual arts. ERIC HORAN

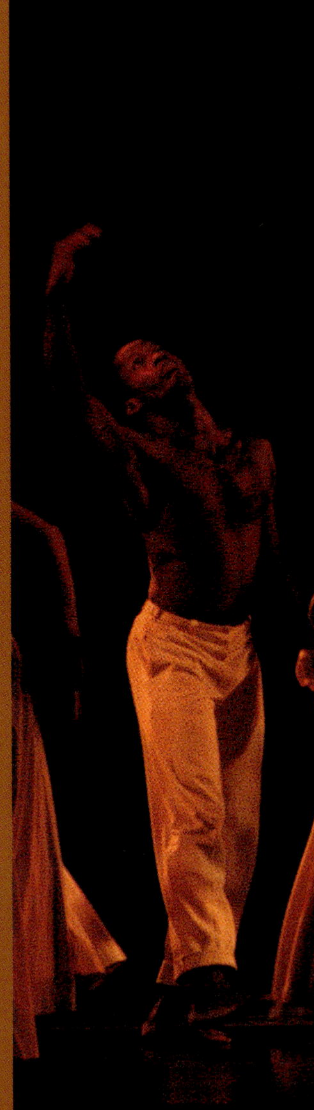

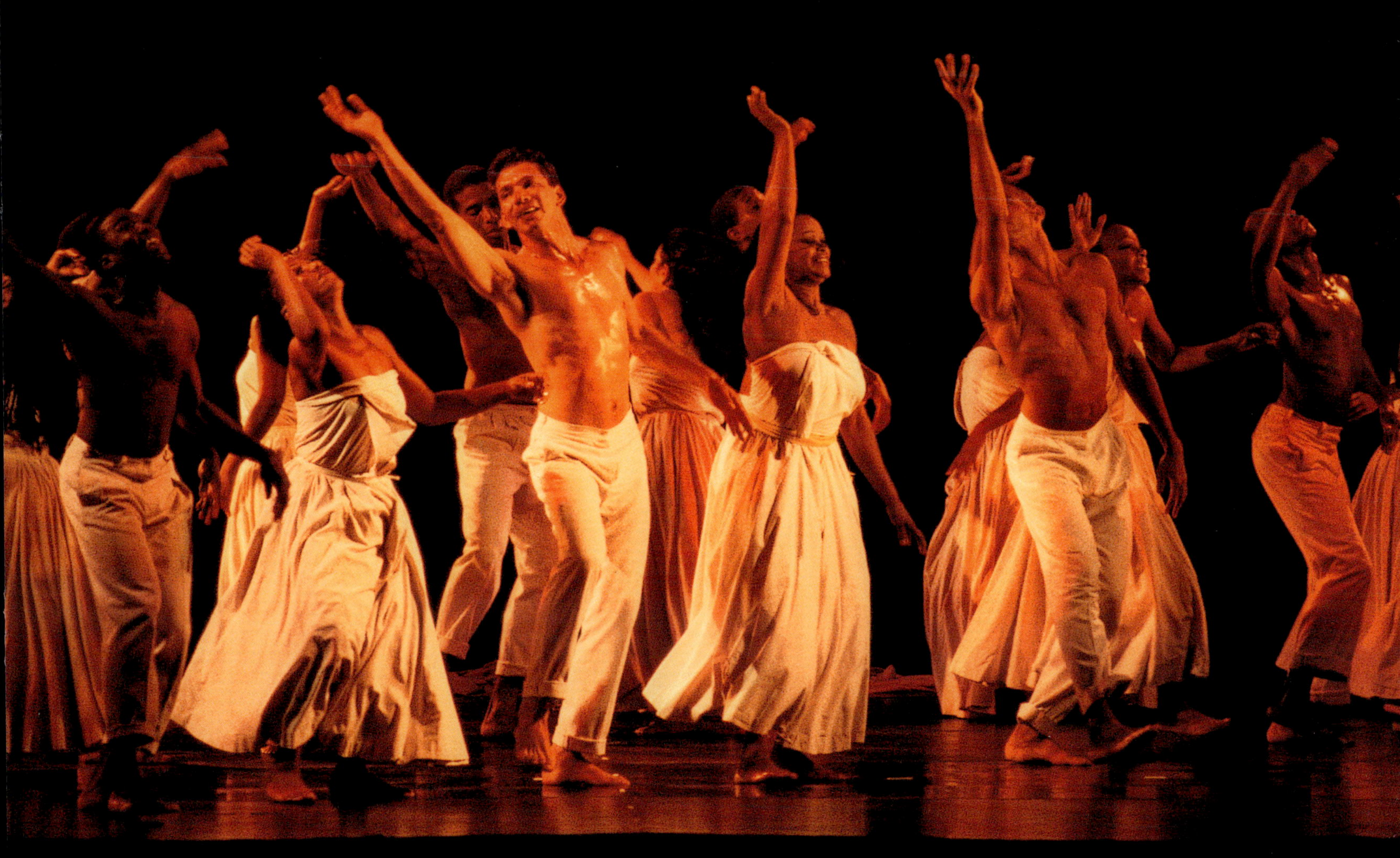

An attraction at a recent Spoleto Festival was the Conjunto Folklorico Nacional de Cuba, performing traditional Afro-Cuban music and dance. International acts are common at Spoleto, which was developed as the U.S. counterpart to the Festival dei Due Mondi (Festival of Two Worlds) in Spoleto, Italy. That festival's founder, composer Gian Carlo Menotti, hand-picked Charleston for the annual event. Eric Horan

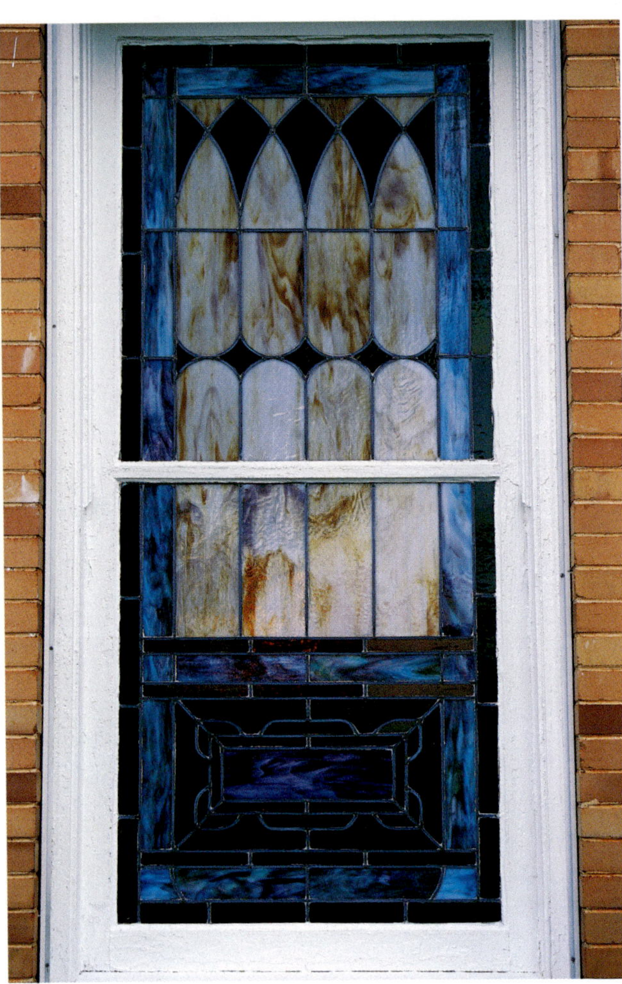

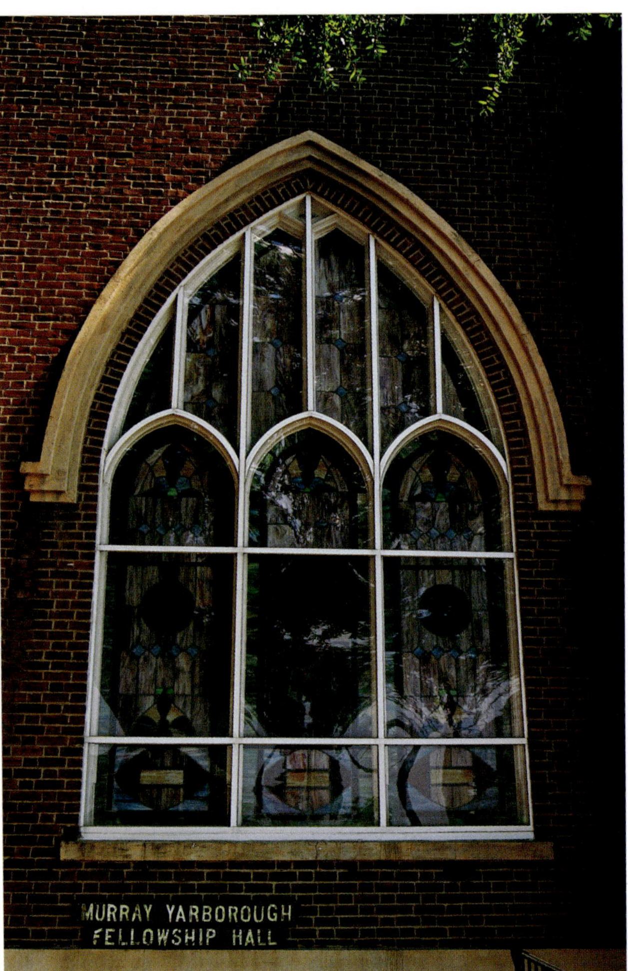

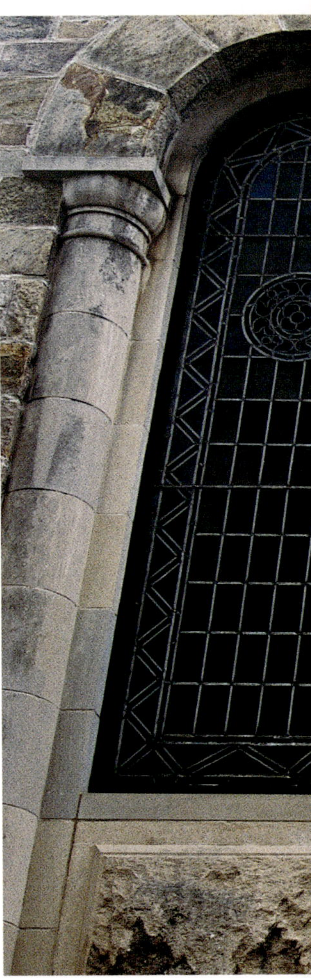

Above left: Colorful stained glass embellishes the Walhalla Presbyterian Church, founded in 1868. Walhalla, county seat of Oconee County on the Georgia border, was named "Garden of the Gods" by its early German inhabitants. Ron Anderson

Above right: A neo-Gothic arch frames the lovely stained glass of the Greene Street United Methodist Church in Columbia. Ron Anderson

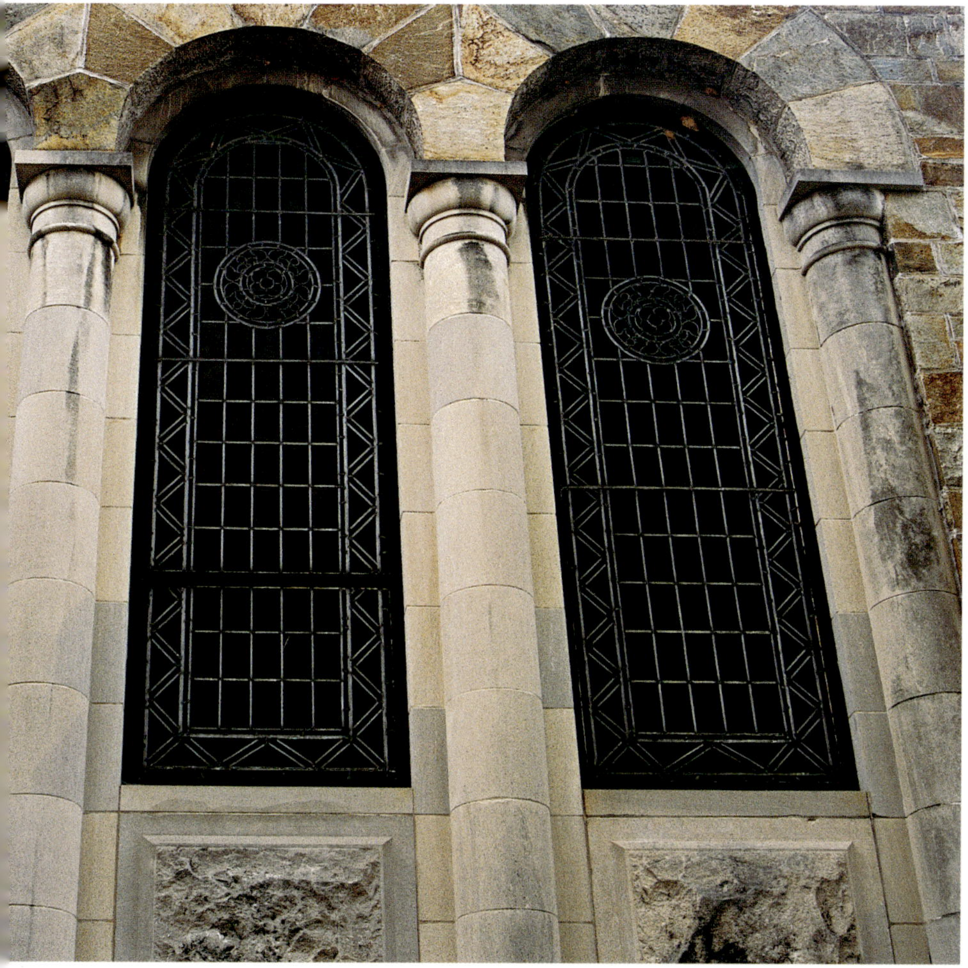

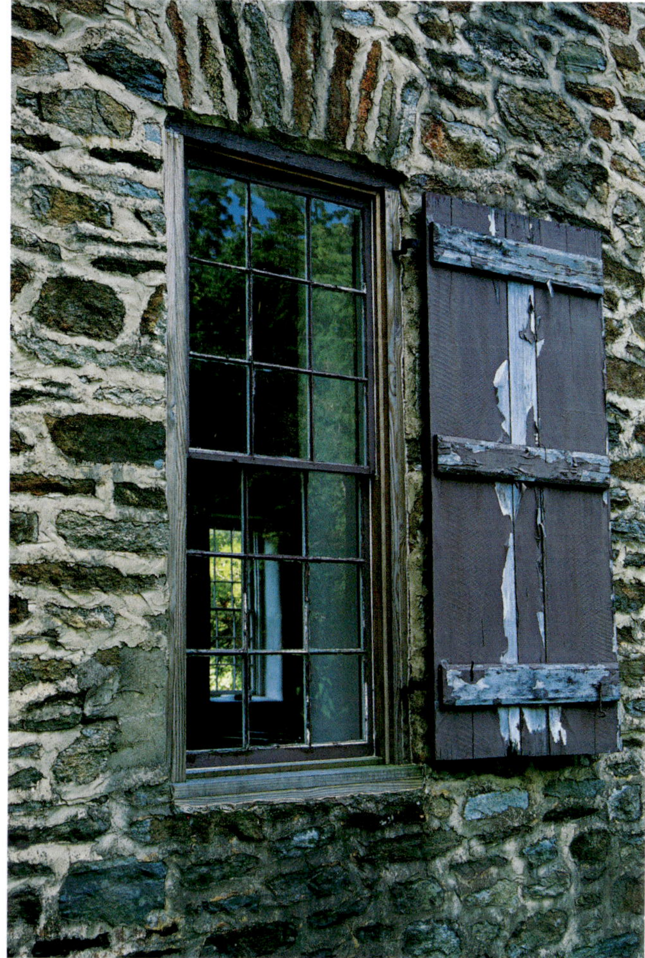

Above left: An elegant trio of windows adorns the First Presbyterian Church of Spartanburg. In 1843, a small group of Presbyterians founded a new congregation in a village then known as Spartanburg Court House. Ron Anderson

Above right: This window provides a glimpse inside the Old Stone Church between Clemson and Pendleton in Pickens County. Originally built in the late 1700s, the structure was damaged by an earthquake around 1900, but was eventually reconstructed in the 1960s. Open to the public, it sees at least one wedding a week year-round. Ron Anderson

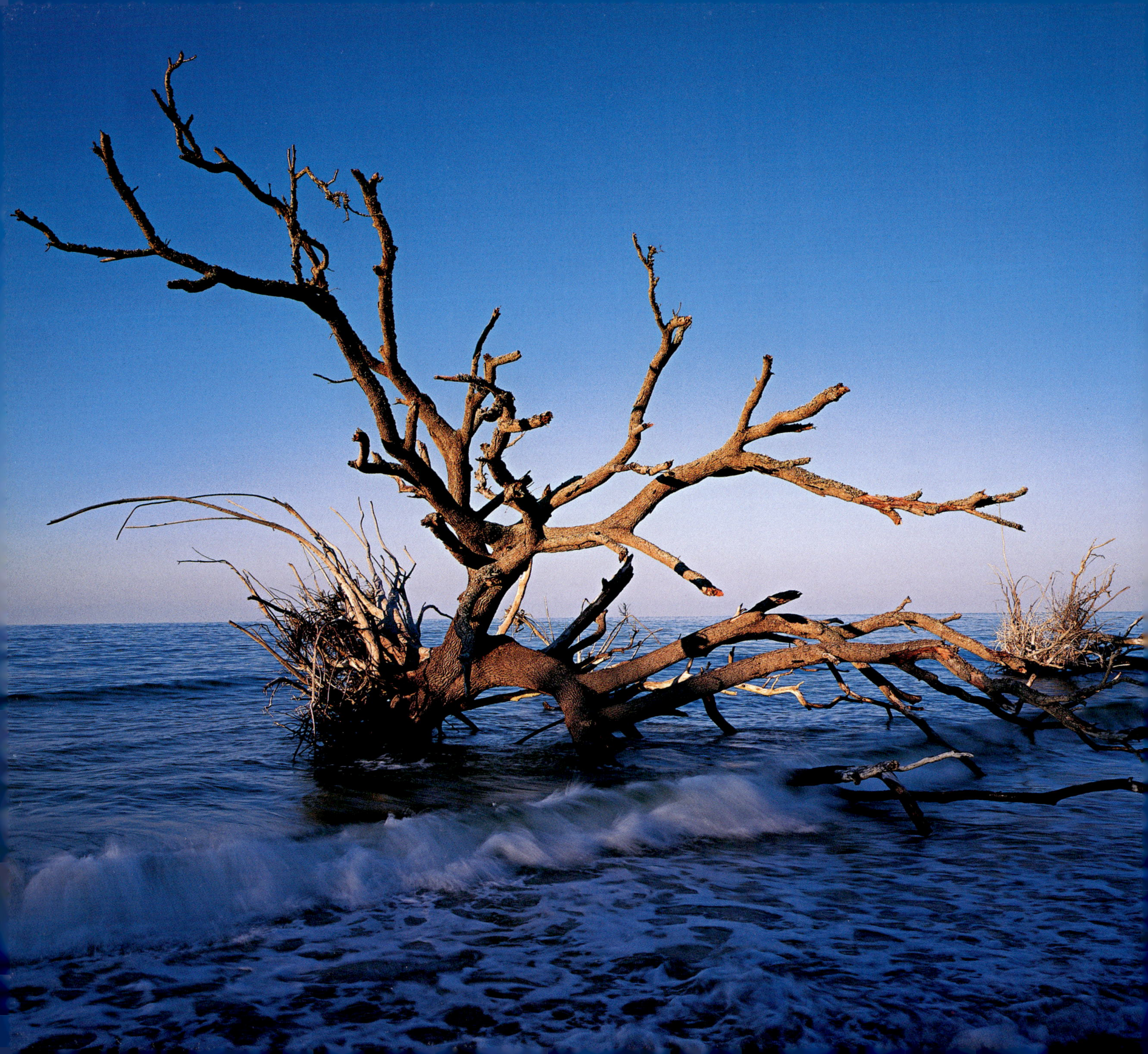

Left: Bay Point Island, accessible today only by boat or air, has served as the site of a Confederate fort, a World War II Coast Guard outpost, and a watch station guarding against marauding pirates. It also attracted plantation families seeking an escape from the heat of the inland summer. Today it is privately owned. Eric Horan

Below: Two airborne ballet dancers find that the world is their stage. Eric Horan

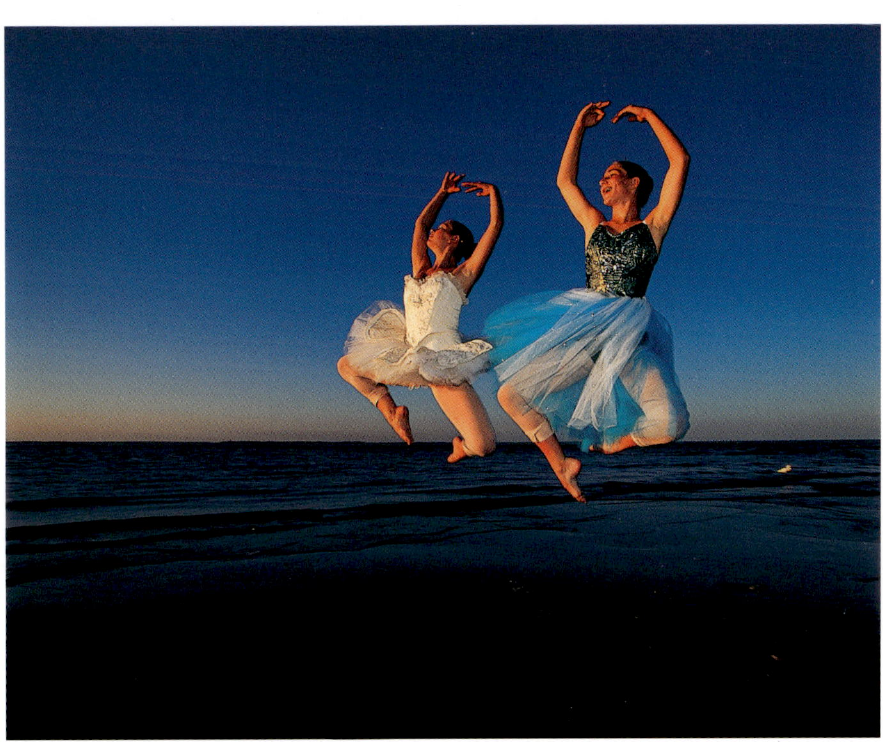

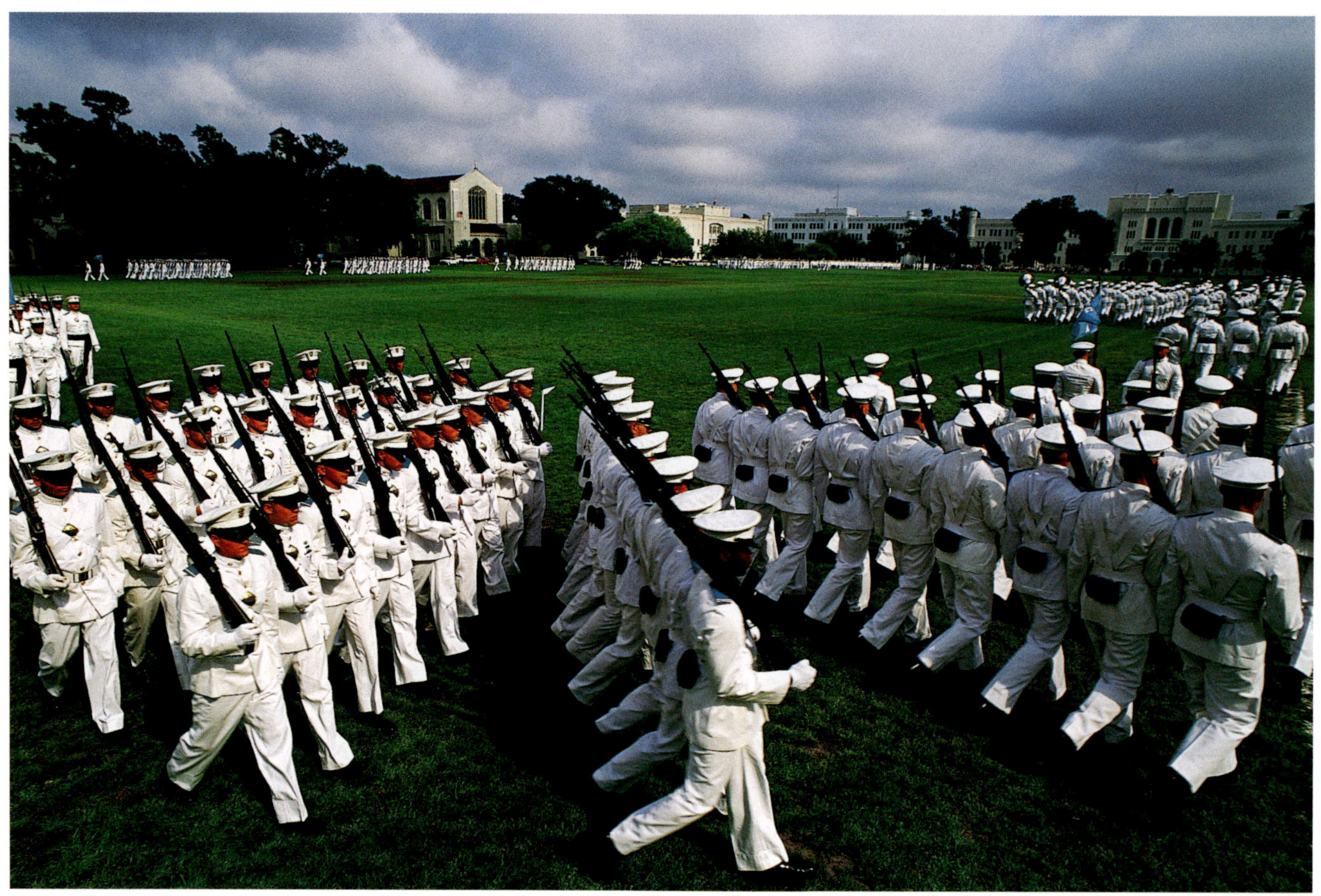

Above: A dress parade makes its measured way across the grounds of The Citadel, the military college of South Carolina. In 1822, the state legislature passed an act establishing a municipal military presence, and by 1829 the original building was constructed on the north end of Marion Square in Charleston. The academy itself was established in December 1842. Eric Horan

Facing page: Citadel cadets stroll around the barracks on campus. In 1865 Union troops occupied the site and burned one of its flagship buildings, and the college didn't reopen until 1882. The structures we see today weren't developed until 1922, when the school outgrew its original site and moved to 176 acres on the Ashley River. Eric Horan

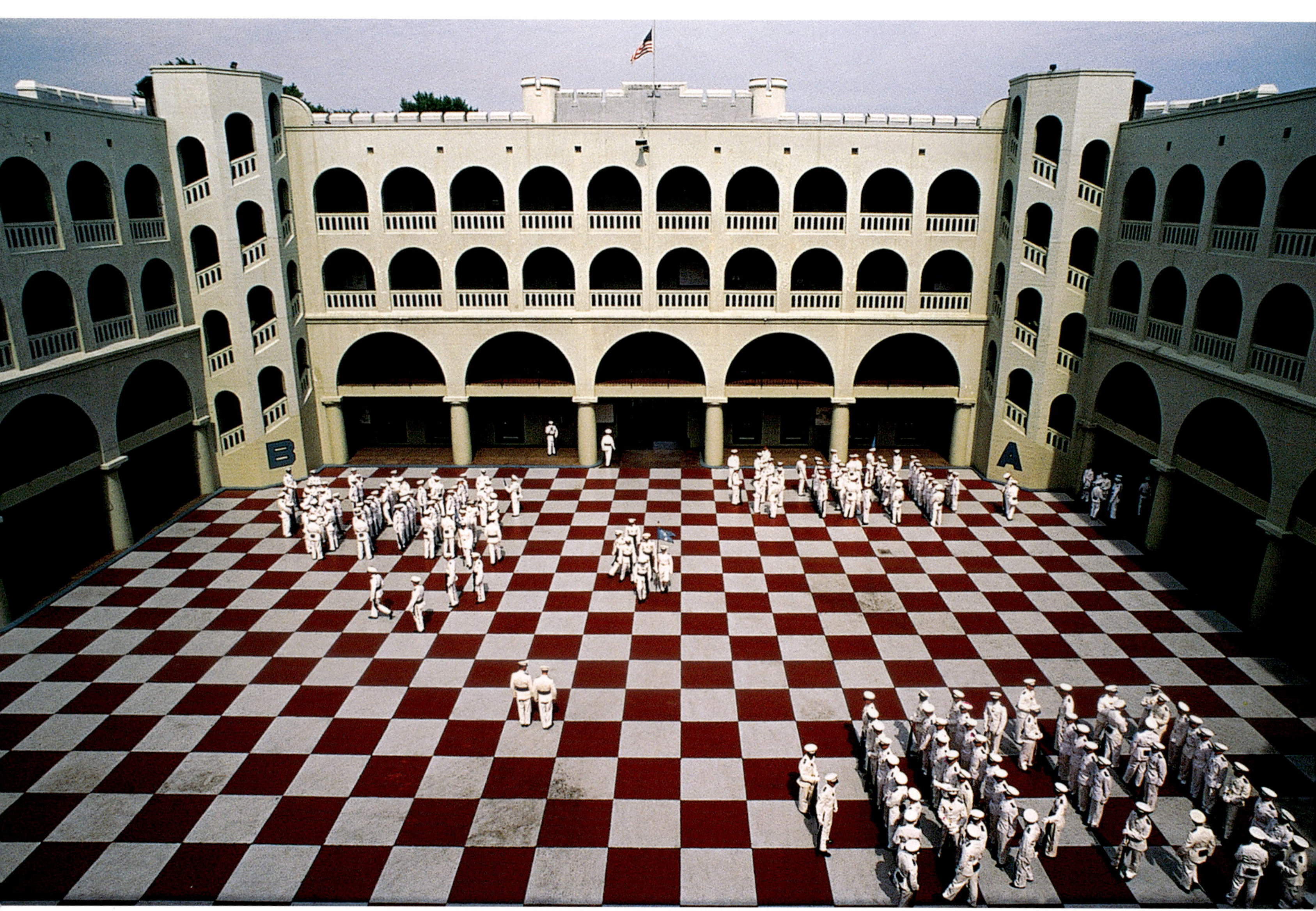
B
A

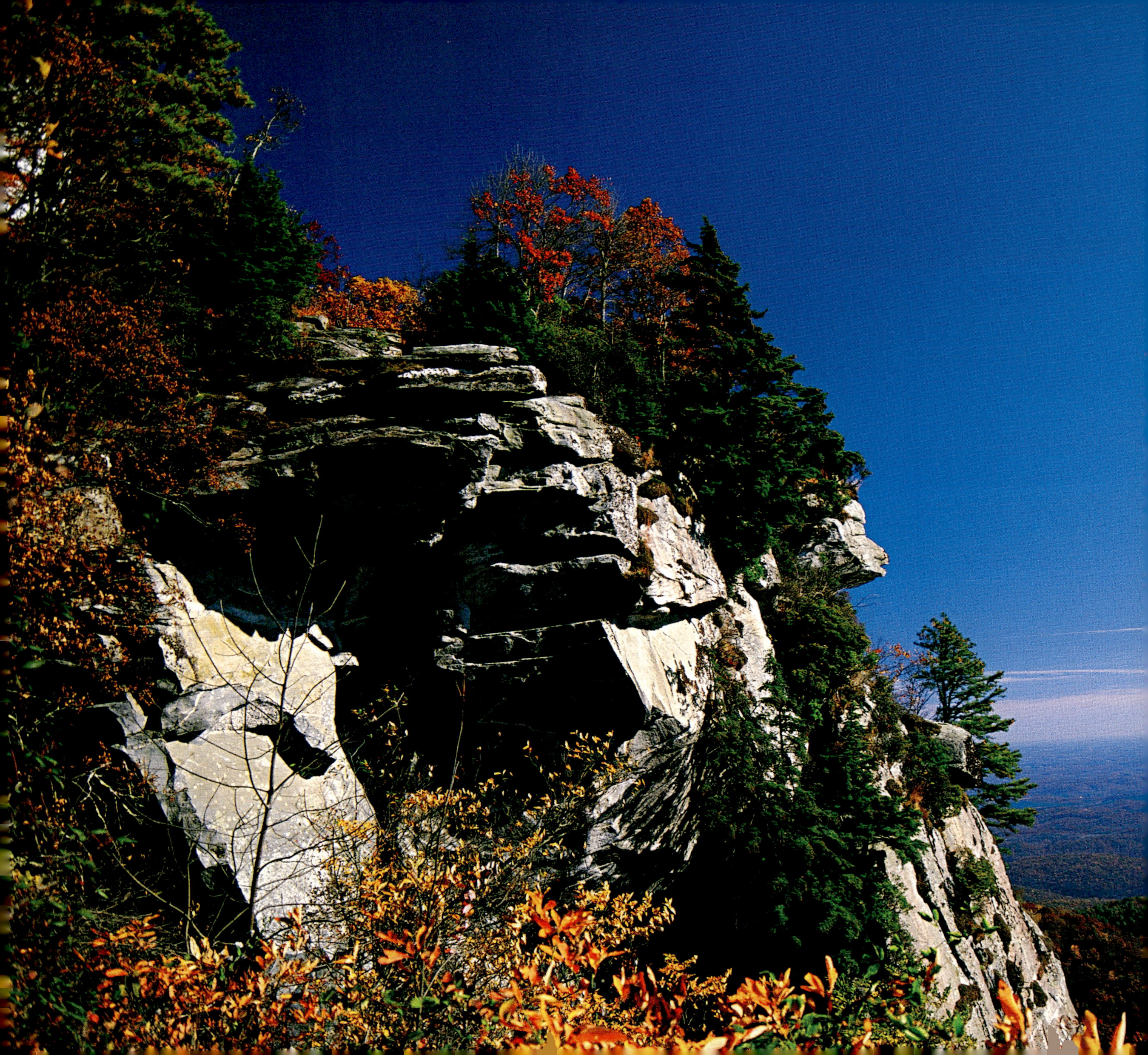

Left: At 3,266 feet above sea level, the Caesars Head overlook offers a panoramic view of Table Rock and other Blue Ridge Mountain peaks. Caesars Head State Park in Greenville County contains 7,500 acres and is much visited during the height of autumn color. Ron Anderson

Below: At roughly 420 feet, Raven Cliff Falls is one of the highest waterfalls in the eastern United States and a main attraction at Caesars Head State Park. Ron Anderson

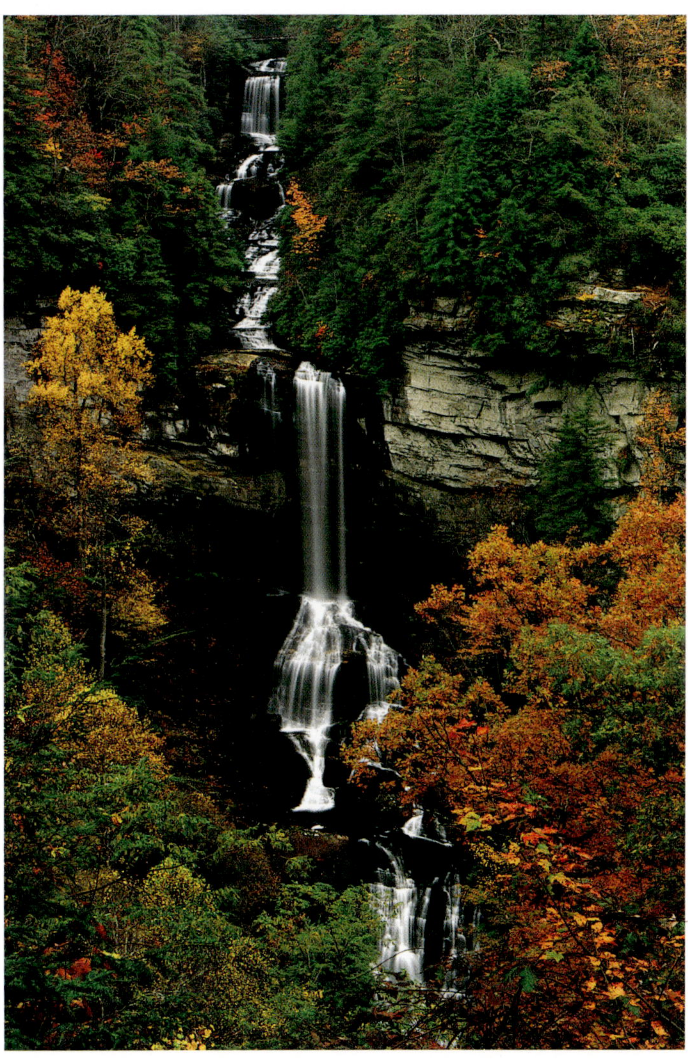

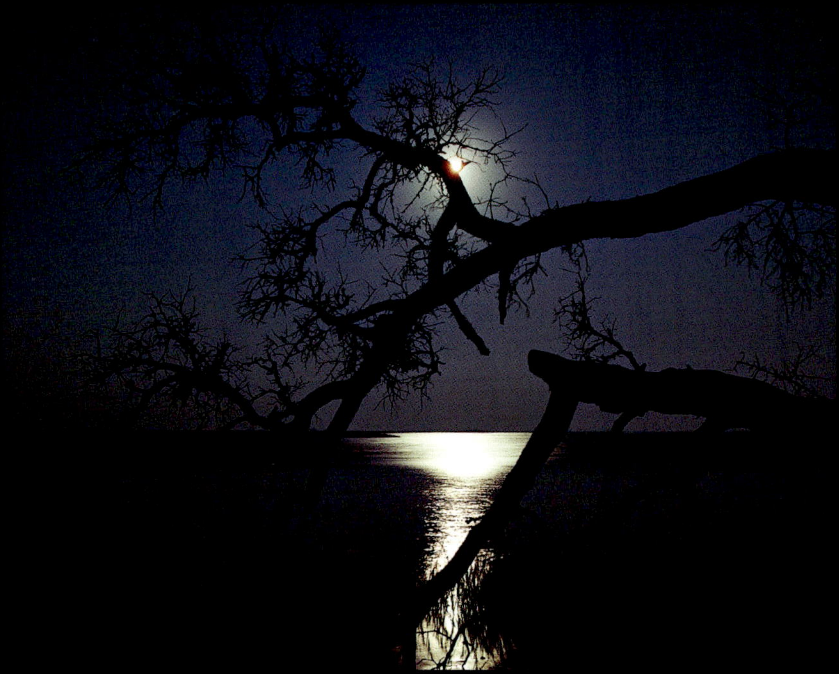

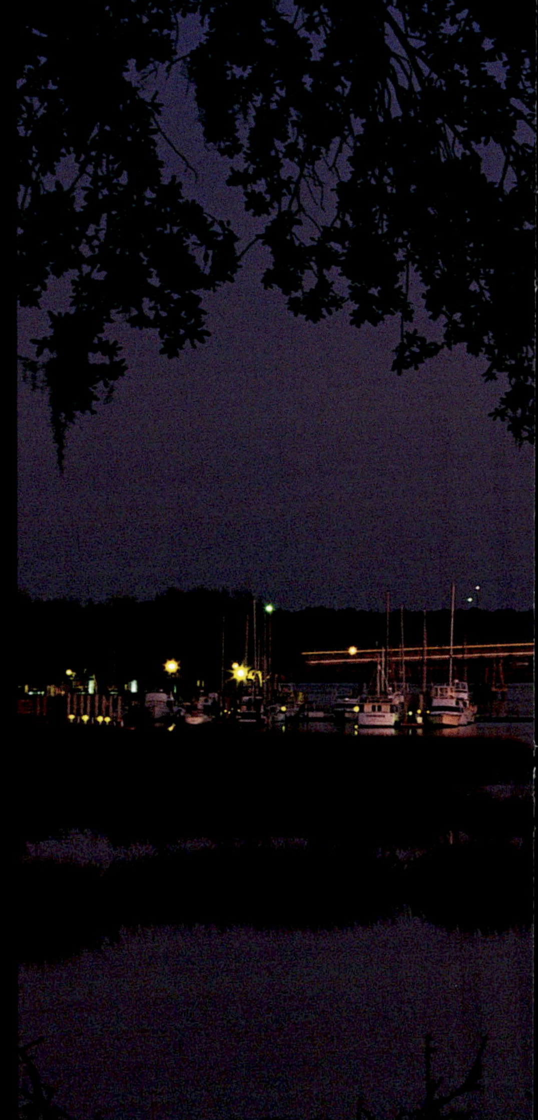

Above: A tree provides a moonlit silhouette over calm waters. Eric Horan

Right: Twilight offers a reflective study of the Woods Memorial Bridge, connecting Beaufort and Lady's Island. Once known as the "Queen of the Carolina Sea Islands," Beaufort was explored by the Spanish in 1514 and chartered by the British in 1711. Eric Horan

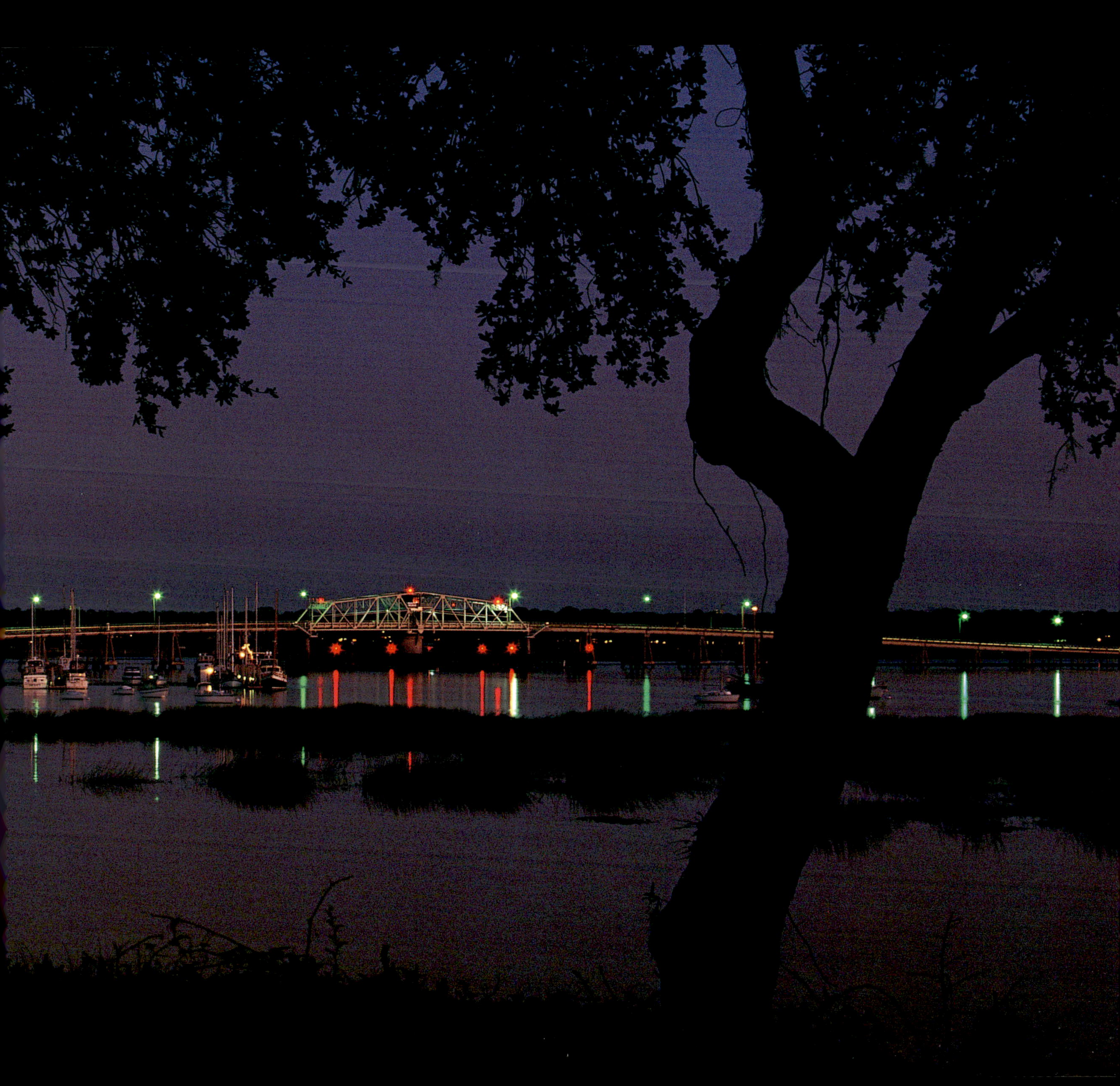

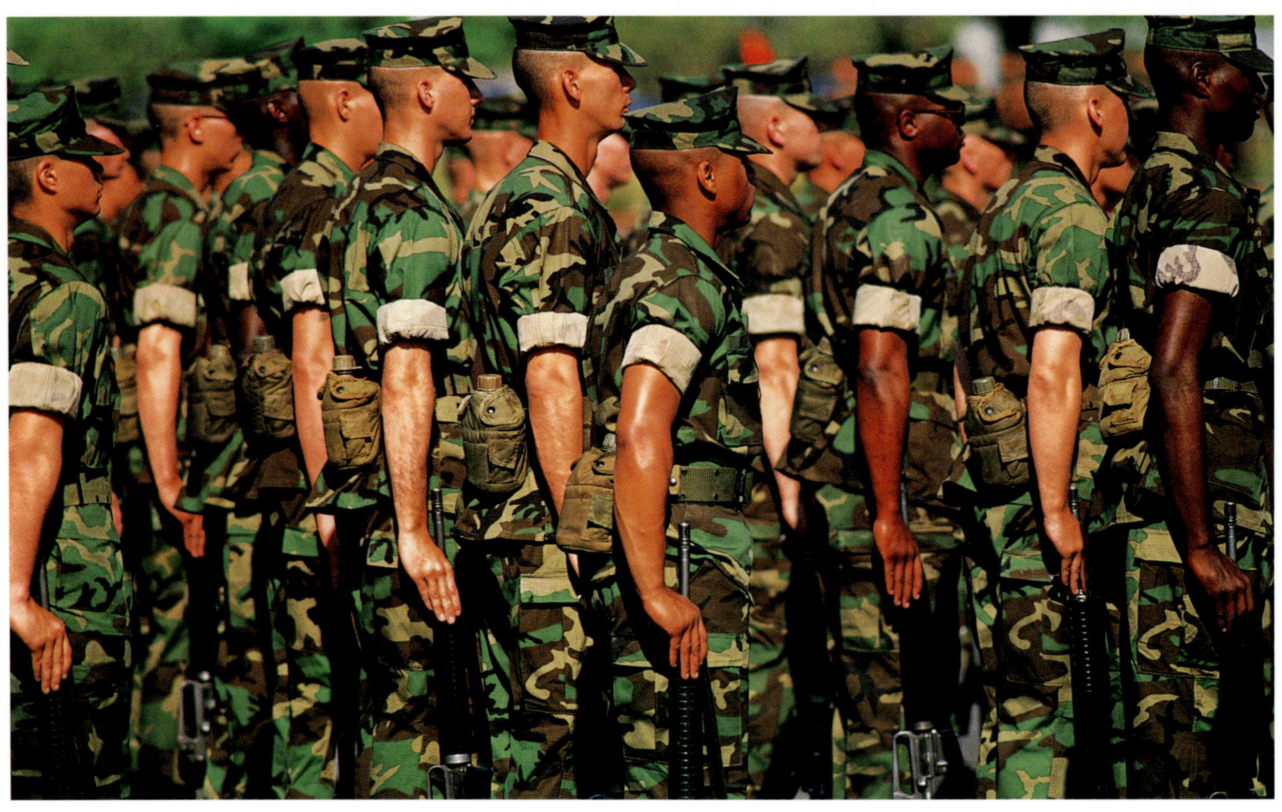

Above: The recruiting and training depot of Parris Island, located off the coast of South Carolina near Beaufort, transforms young men and women into tough U.S. Marines. The island was originally purchased by an Englishman named Colonel Alexander Parris, and plantation life flourished here until the Civil War. Marines were first stationed on Parris Island in 1891. ERIC HORAN

Facing page: Charleston's Southern charm is reflected in a much-admired row of colorful 1750s homes, aptly called Rainbow Row. They were originally owned by merchants who lived in the rooms above their stores. RON ANDERSON

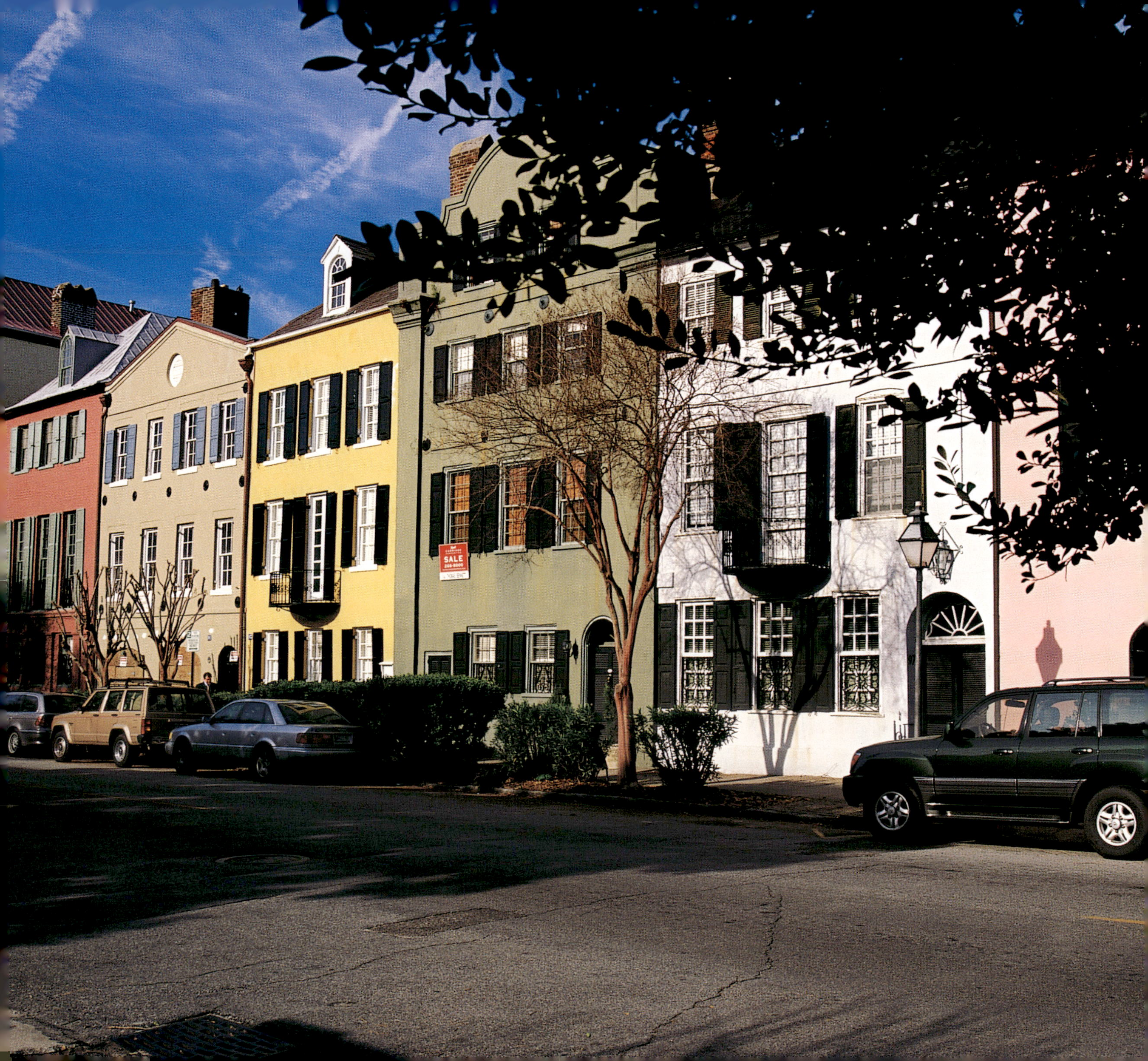
SALE

Right: Shrimp boats settle for the night at the mouth of the Beaufort River at Port Royal Sound. Eric Horan

Below: A shrimper inspects his catch off the Hilton Head coast. Eric Horan

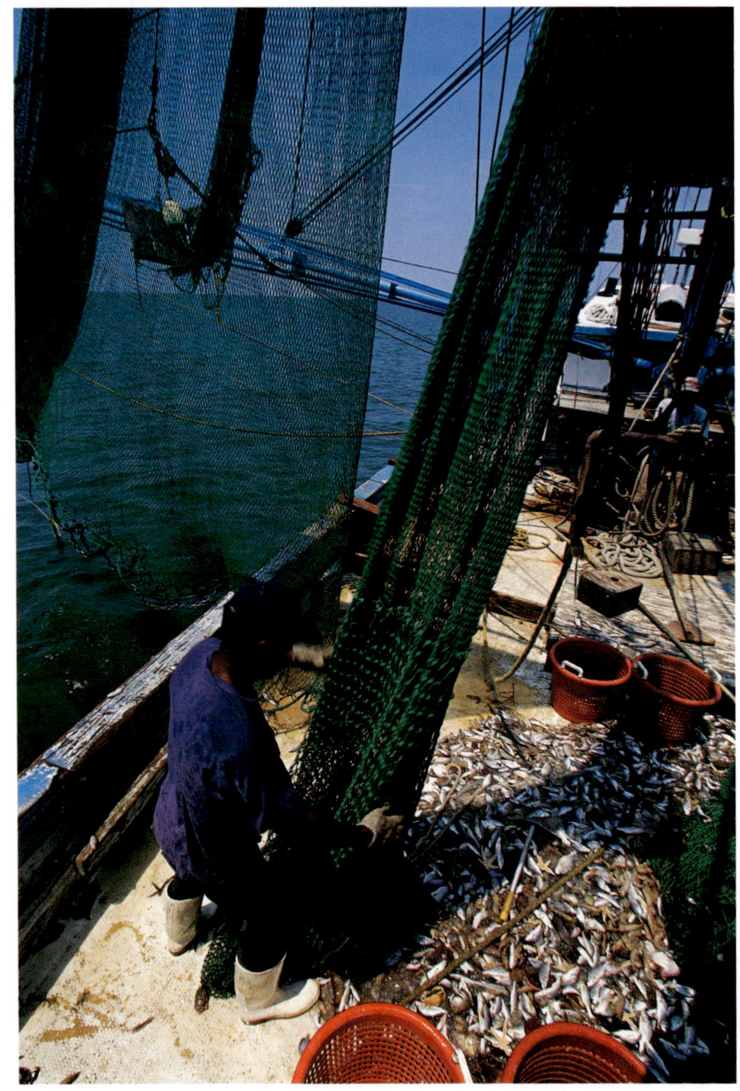

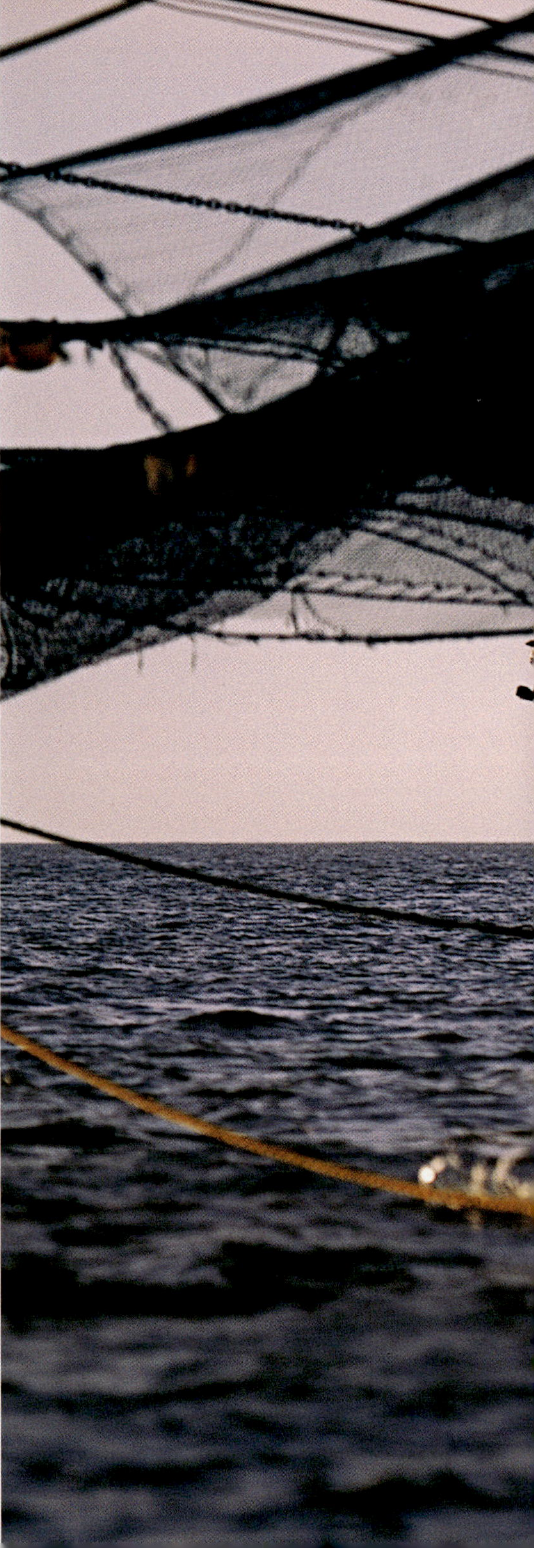

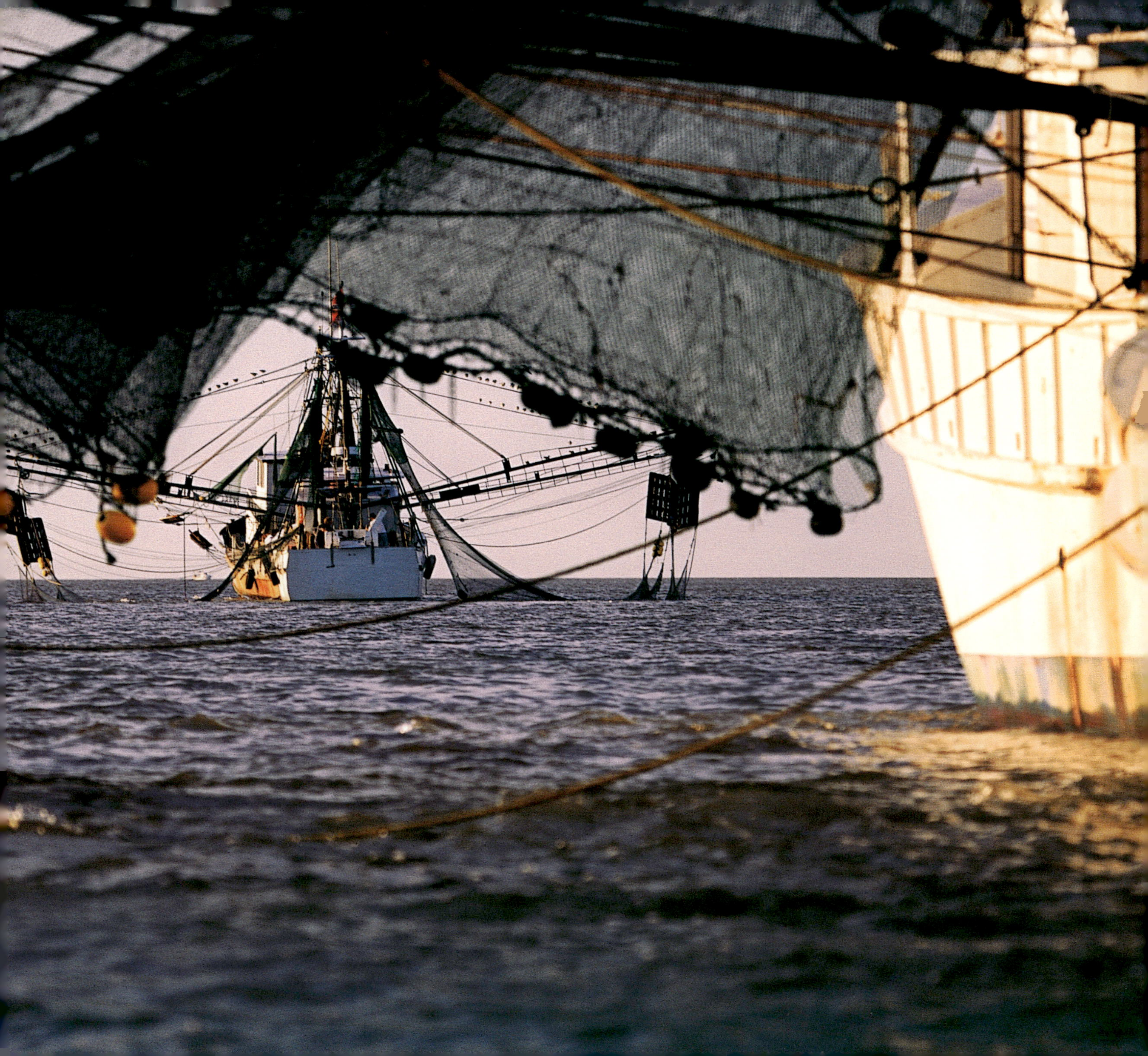

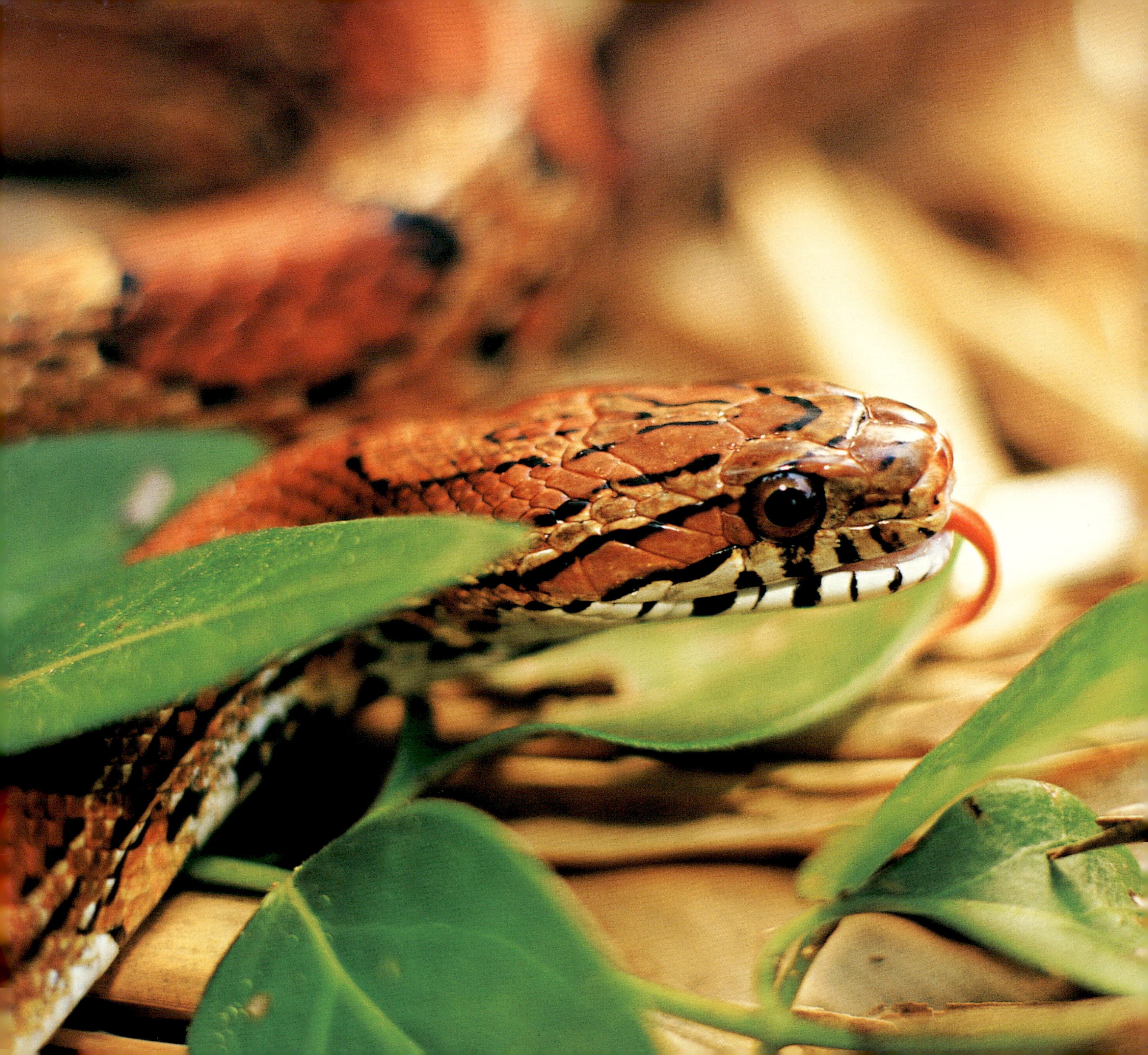

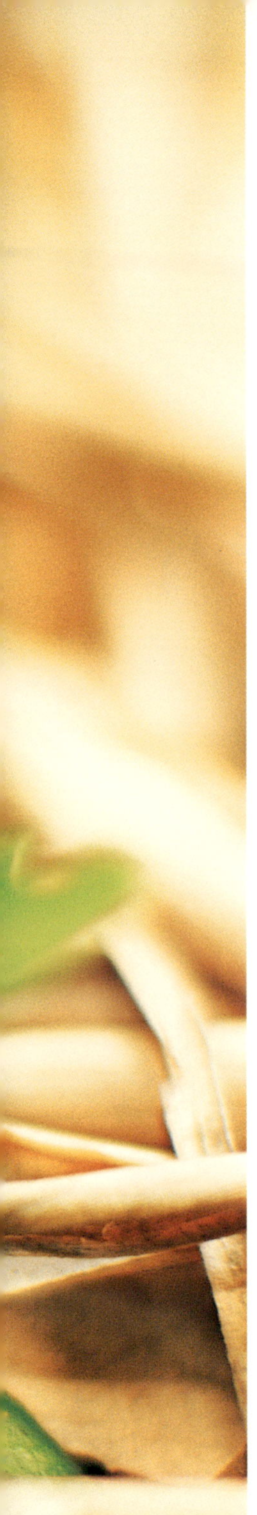

Left: A colorful corn snake seeks refuge among leaves. There are at least four dozen snake species in South Carolina, though only a handful are poisonous. Eric Horan

Below: Loggerhead sea turtles, which have been a threatened species since 1978, take 20 to 30 years to mature and can weigh 800 pounds. Carolina beaches provide important nesting habitats for these massive sea creatures. Eric Horan

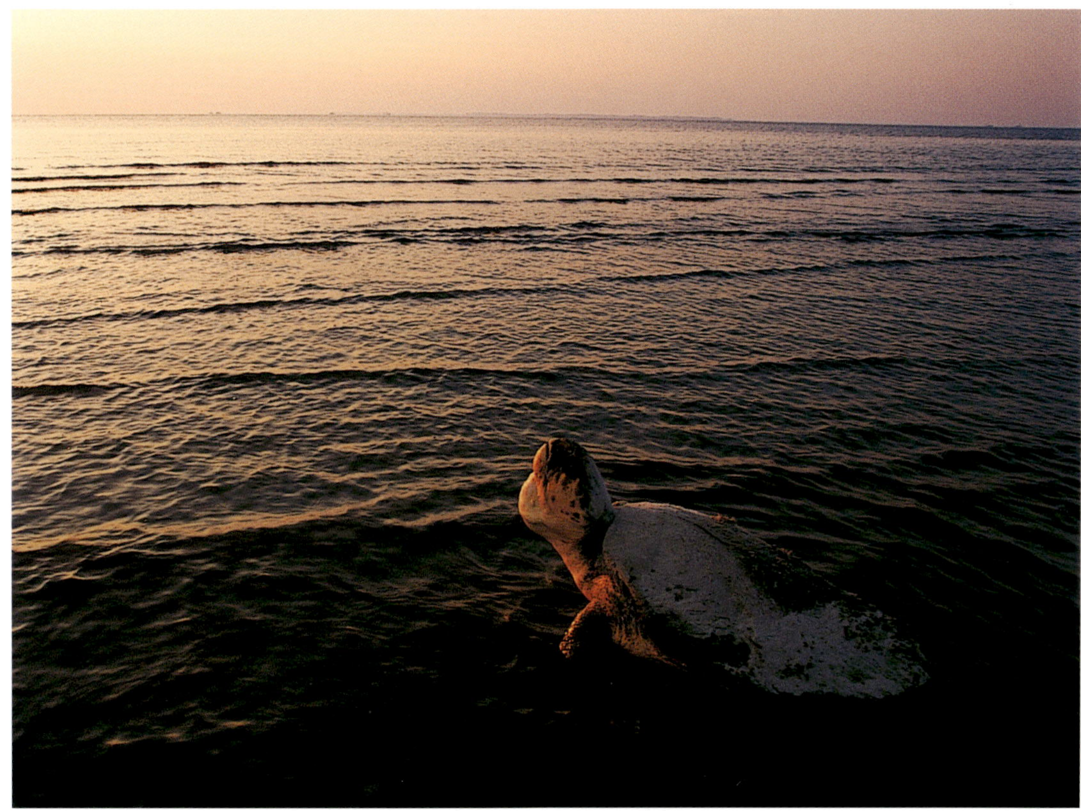

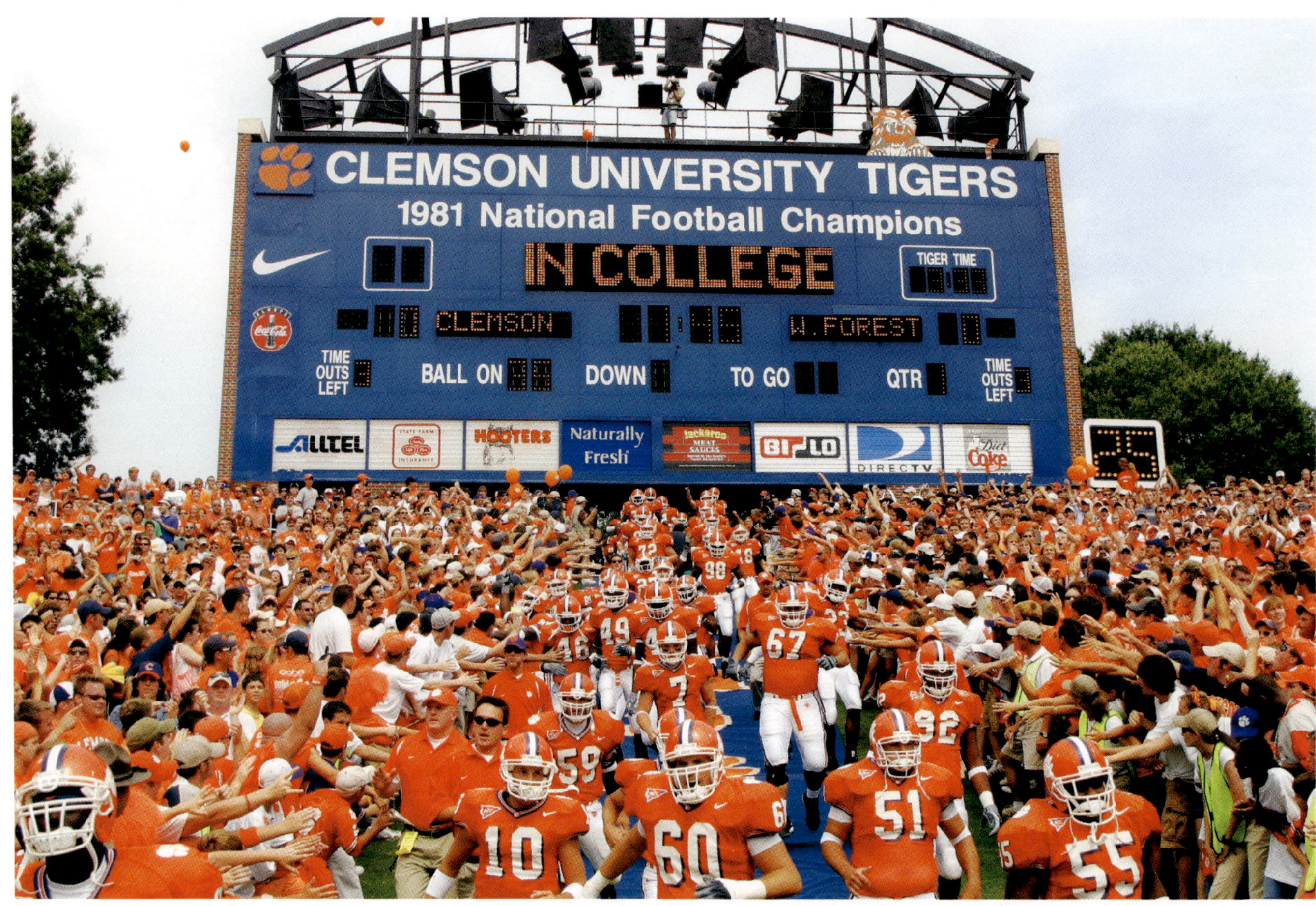

Constructed in 1942, Memorial Stadium is home to the Clemson University Tigers. The late Presbyterian College coach Lonnie McMillan dubbed it "Death Valley," a nickname fans relish and teams facing the ruthless Tigers dread.
PHOTO COURTESY OF ROY PHILPOTT FOR THE CLEMSON UNIVERSITY TIGERS

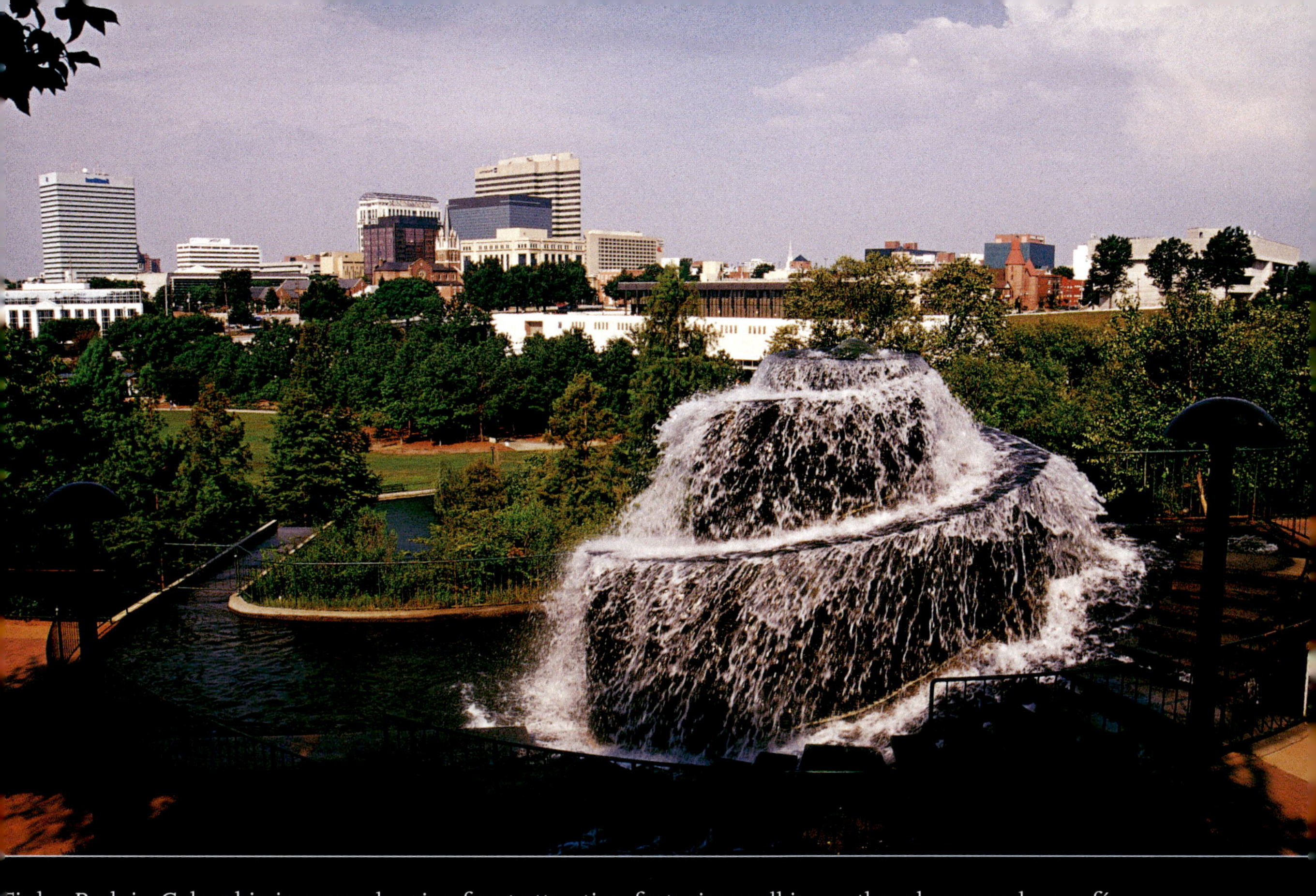

Finlay Park in Columbia is a popular riverfront attraction featuring walking paths, playgrounds, a café, annual festivals, and live performances. It also offers a nice panorama of the capital city's downtown. Ron Anderson

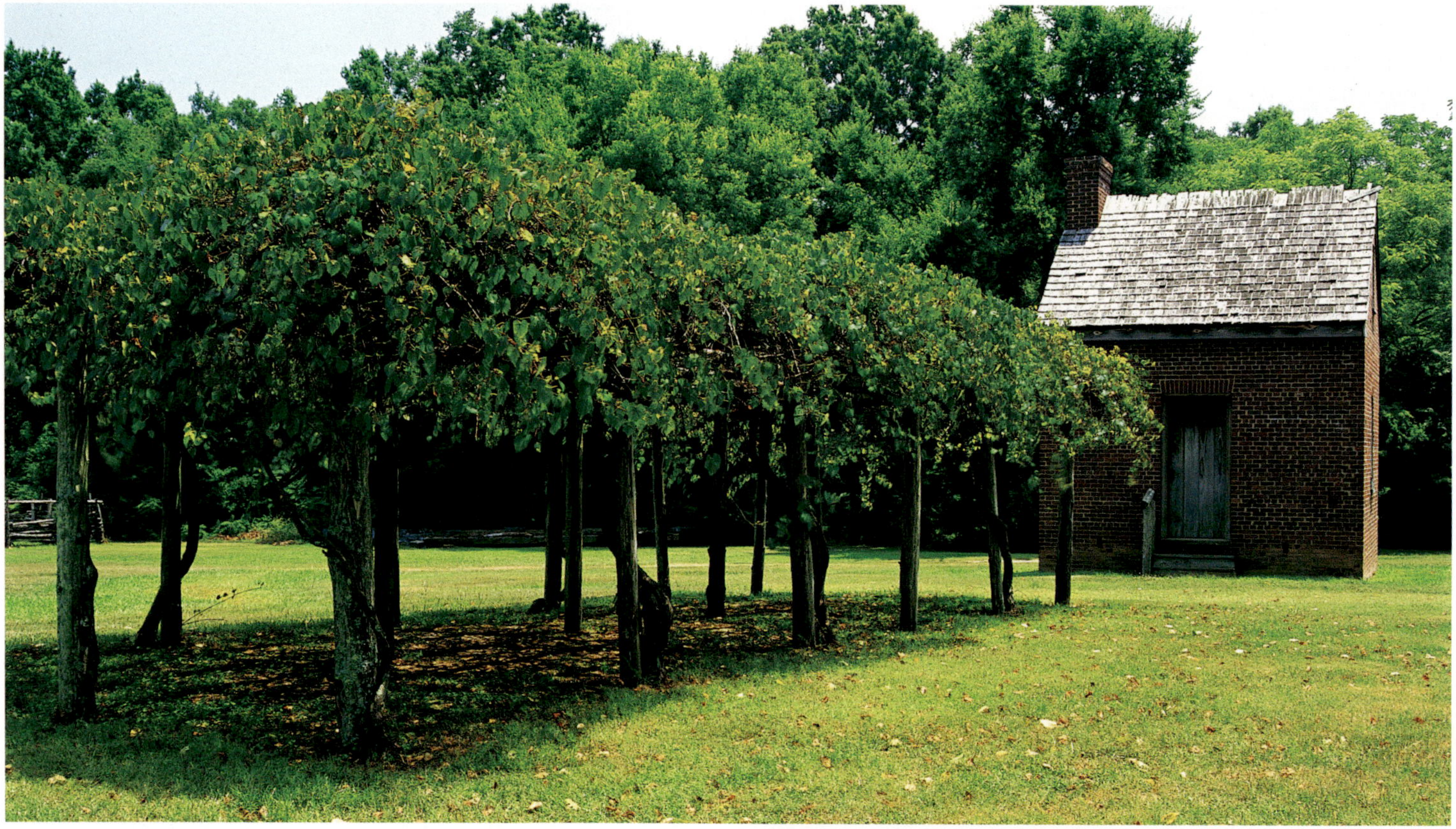

Above: Remnants of the cotton plantation run by John and Harriet Bratton, including a working orchard and brick slave dwellings, make up part of Brattonsville, a 775-acre historic site near Rock Hill. RON ANDERSON

Right: Constructed between 1823 and 1826, this imposing home, known as the Homestead, belonged to Dr. John Bratton and his wife Harriet. The side wings and Greek Revival porch were later additions to the house. After Dr. Bratton died in 1843, Harriet continued to manage the large plantation with the help of her son. RON ANDERSON

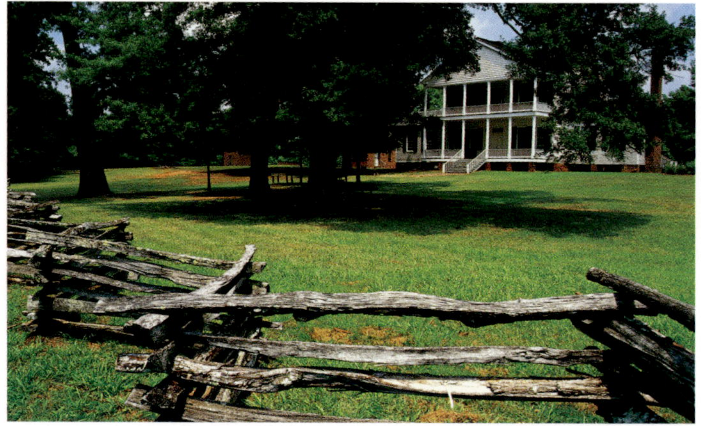

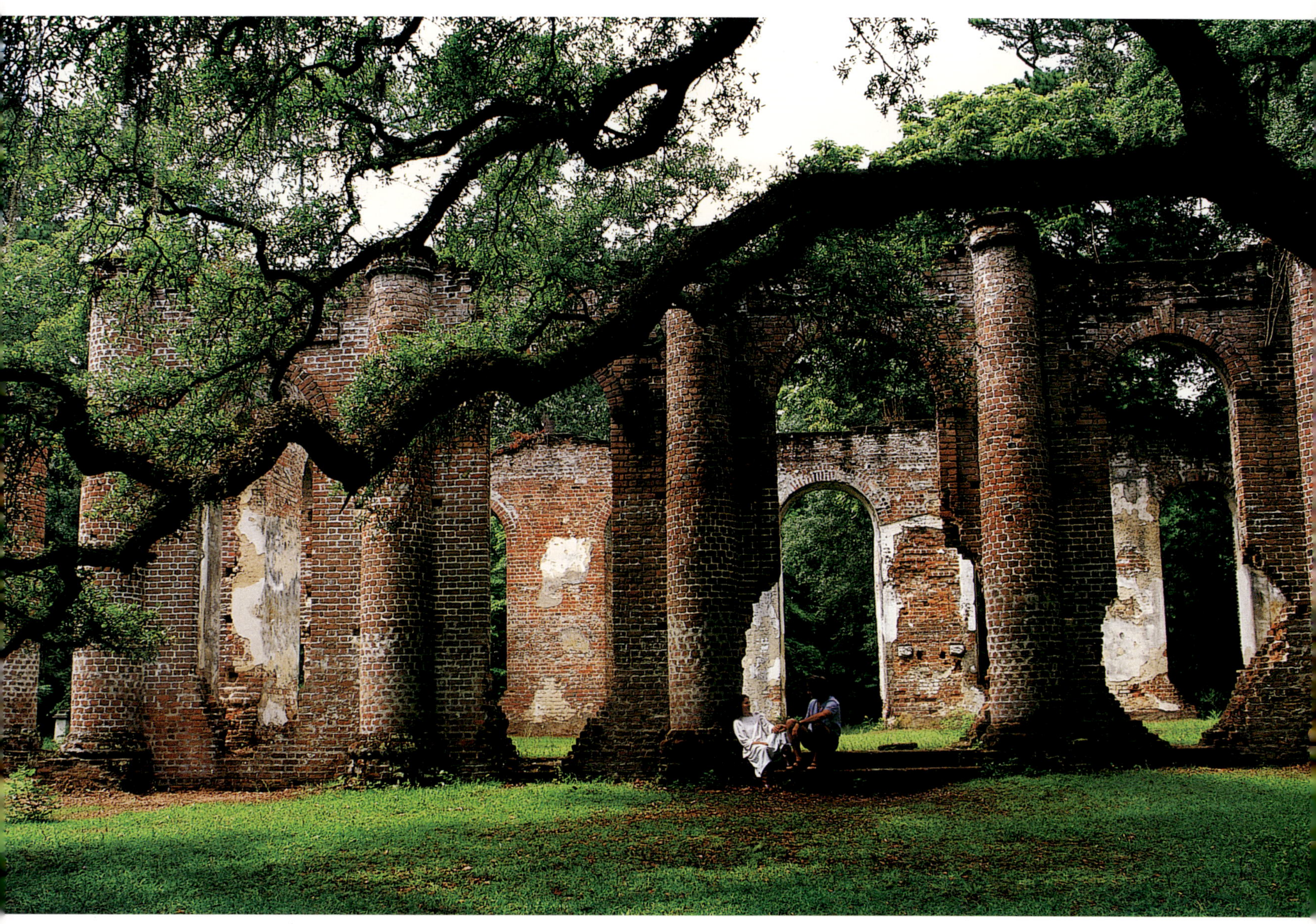

Above: Originally built between 1745 and 1757 by a plantation owner, Old Sheldon Church near Beaufort was burned by British troops in 1779, rebuilt, then destroyed by Sherman's Union troops in 1865. Despite its violent past, the picturesque Greek Revival ruins today provide a quiet place to reflect. ERIC HORAN

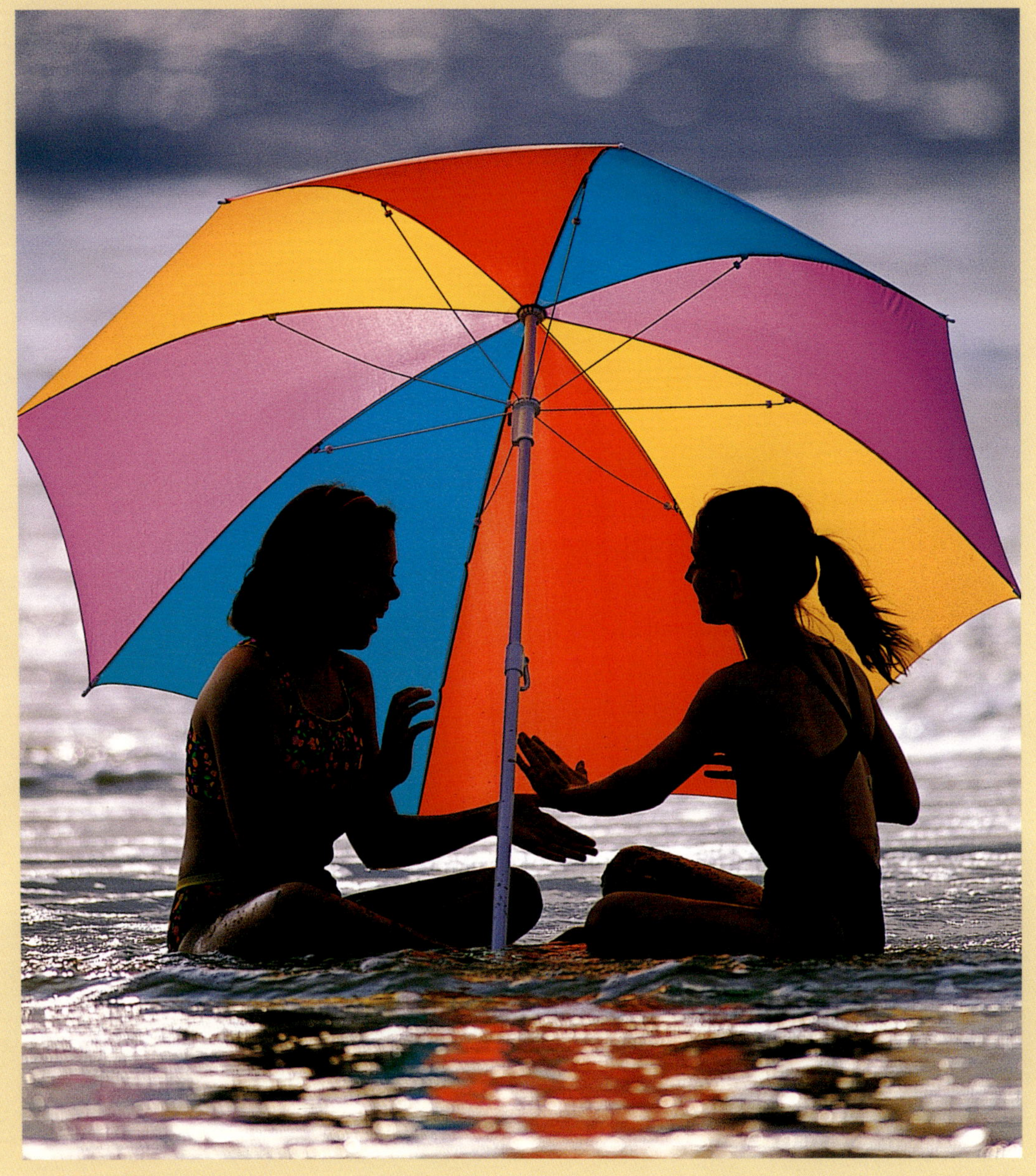

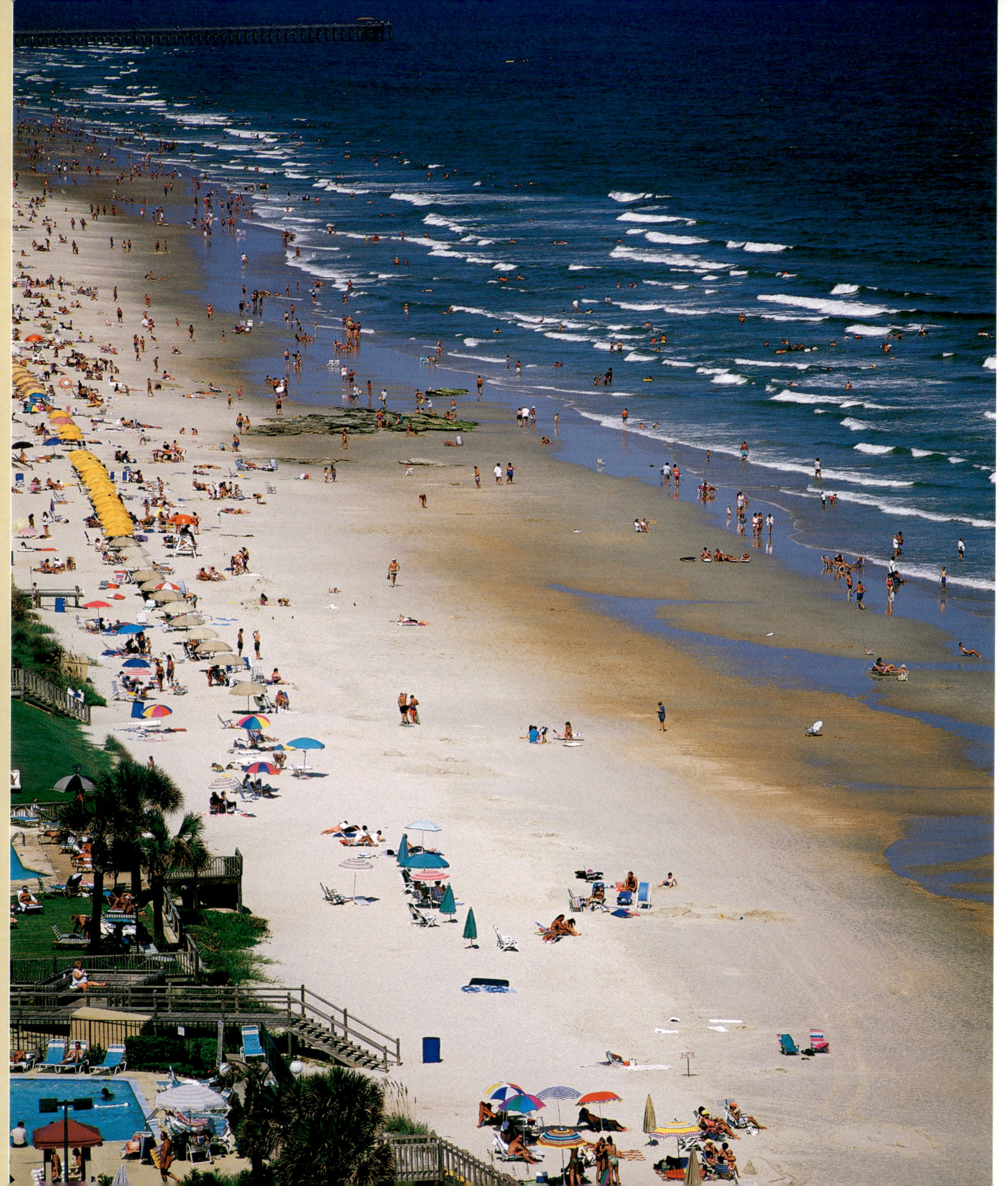

Left: With its wide expanse of beaches, premier golf courses, and nighttime attractions, Myrtle Beach is a well-known destination for vacationers. Eric Horan

Facing page: Two girls at Hilton Head enjoy summer fun under a bright umbrella. Eric Horan

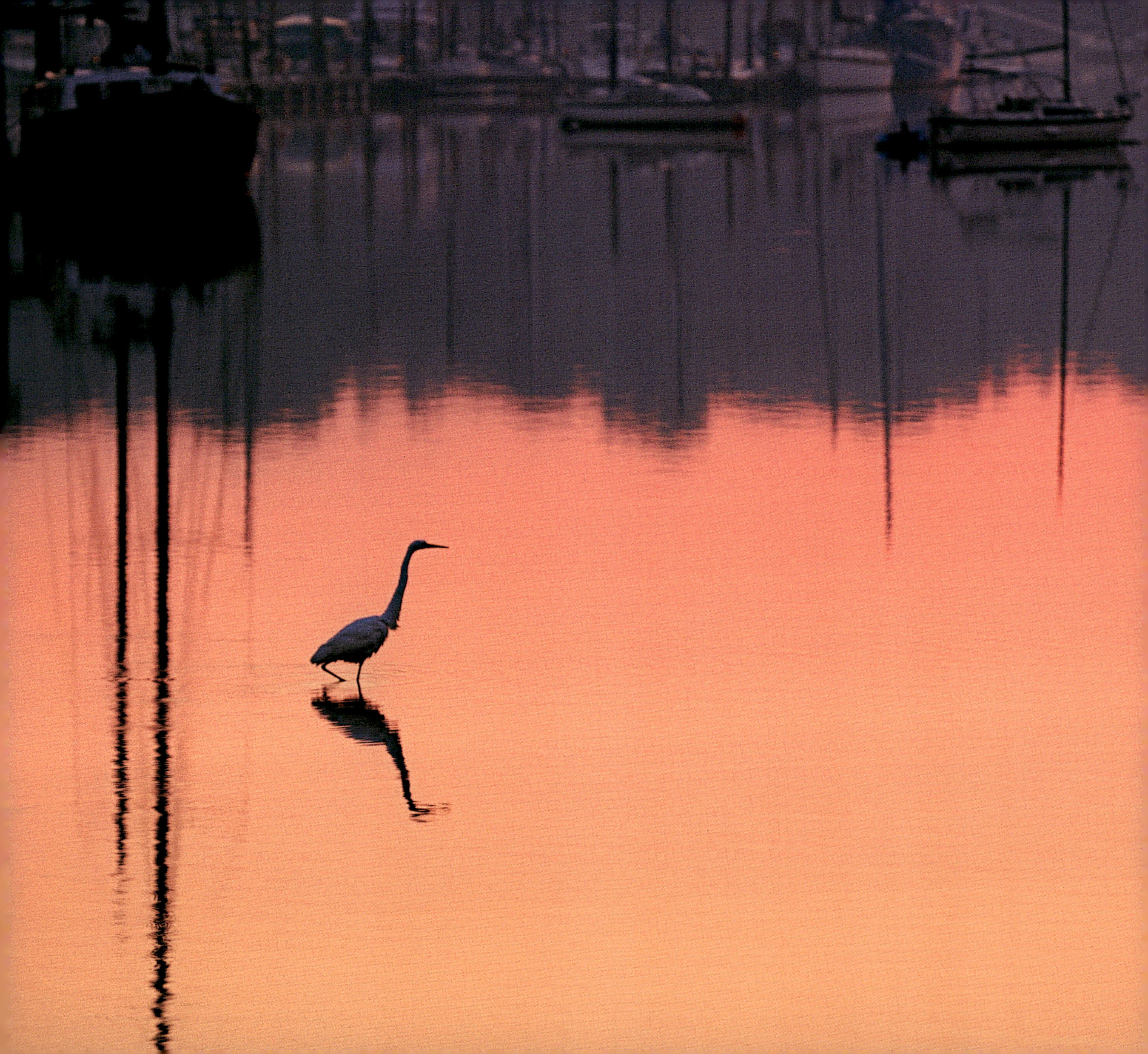

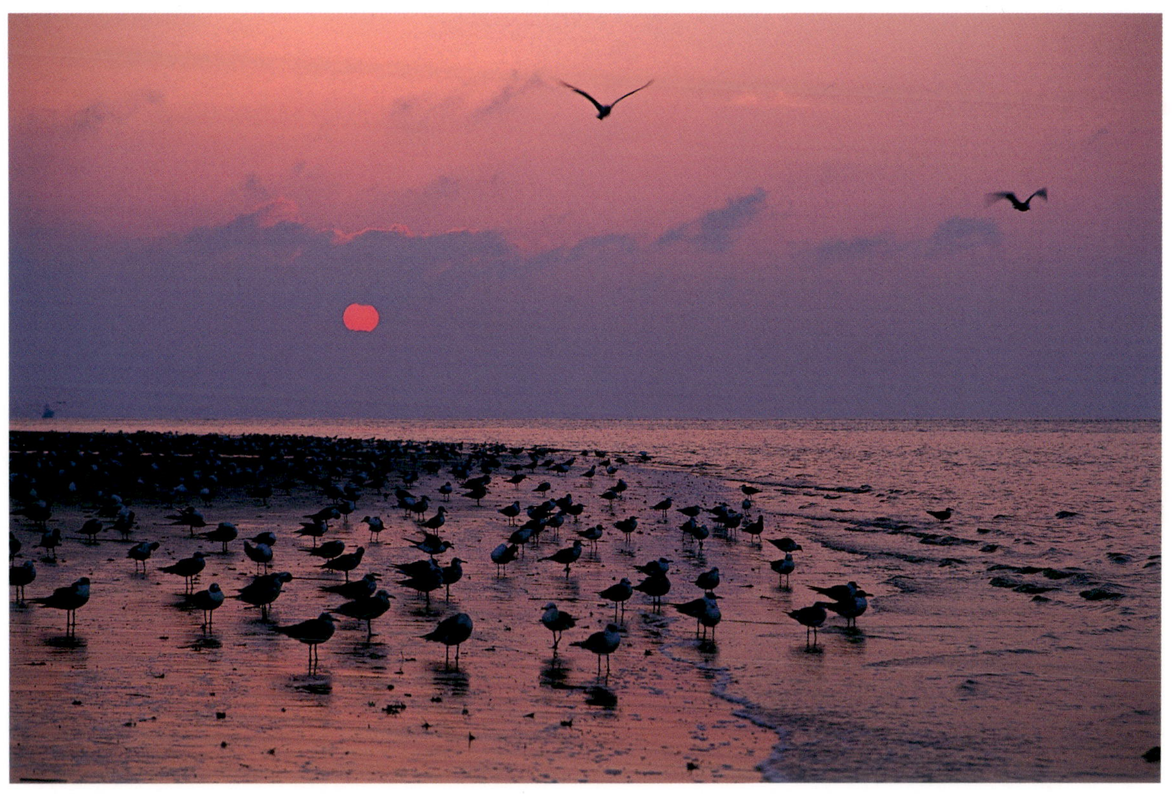

Above: Harbor Island, a barrier island not far from Beaufort, is a unique coastal resort. Eric Horan

Facing page: A great egret trolls for a meal in Lady's Island Marina near Beaufort. Eric Horan

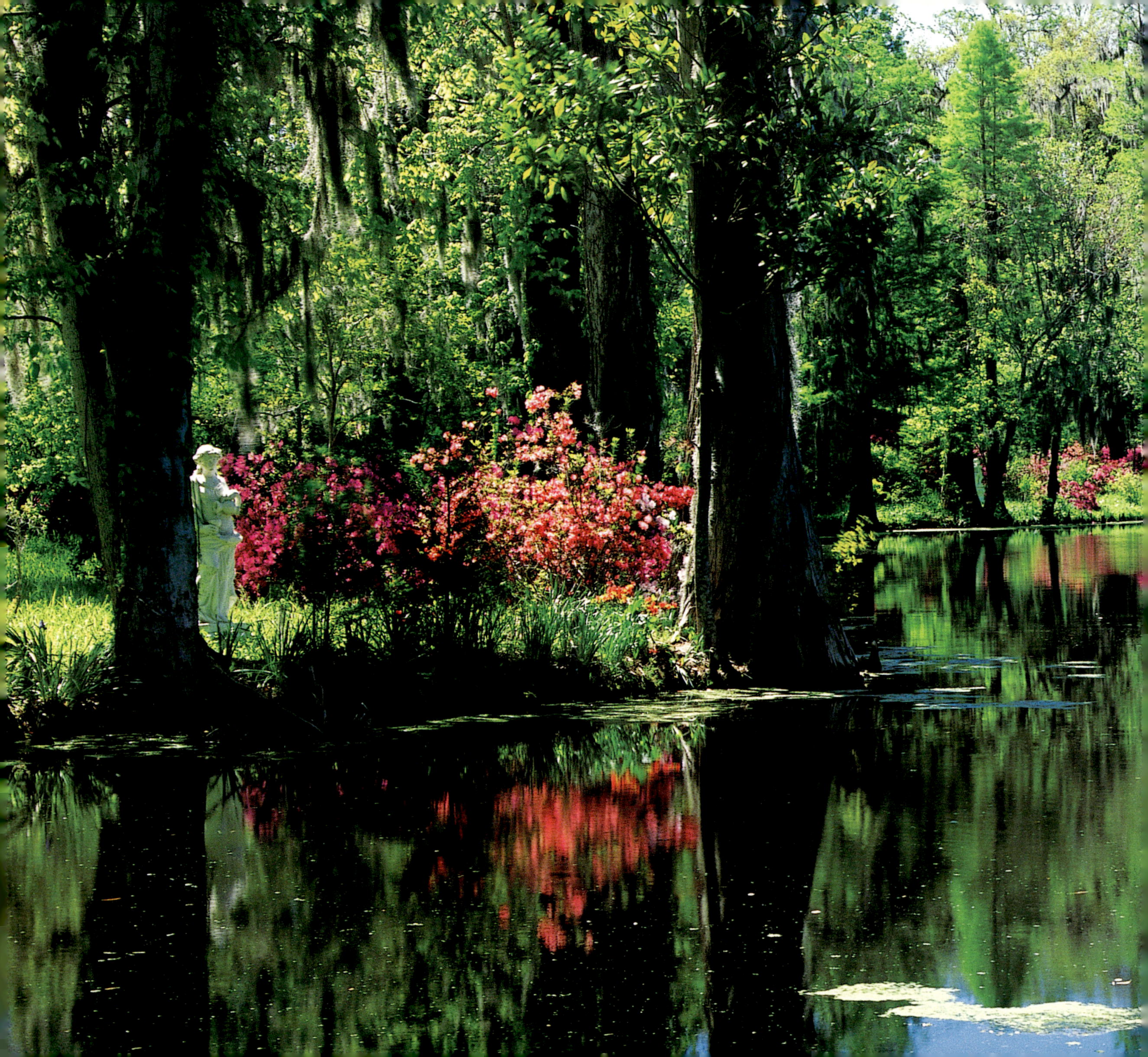

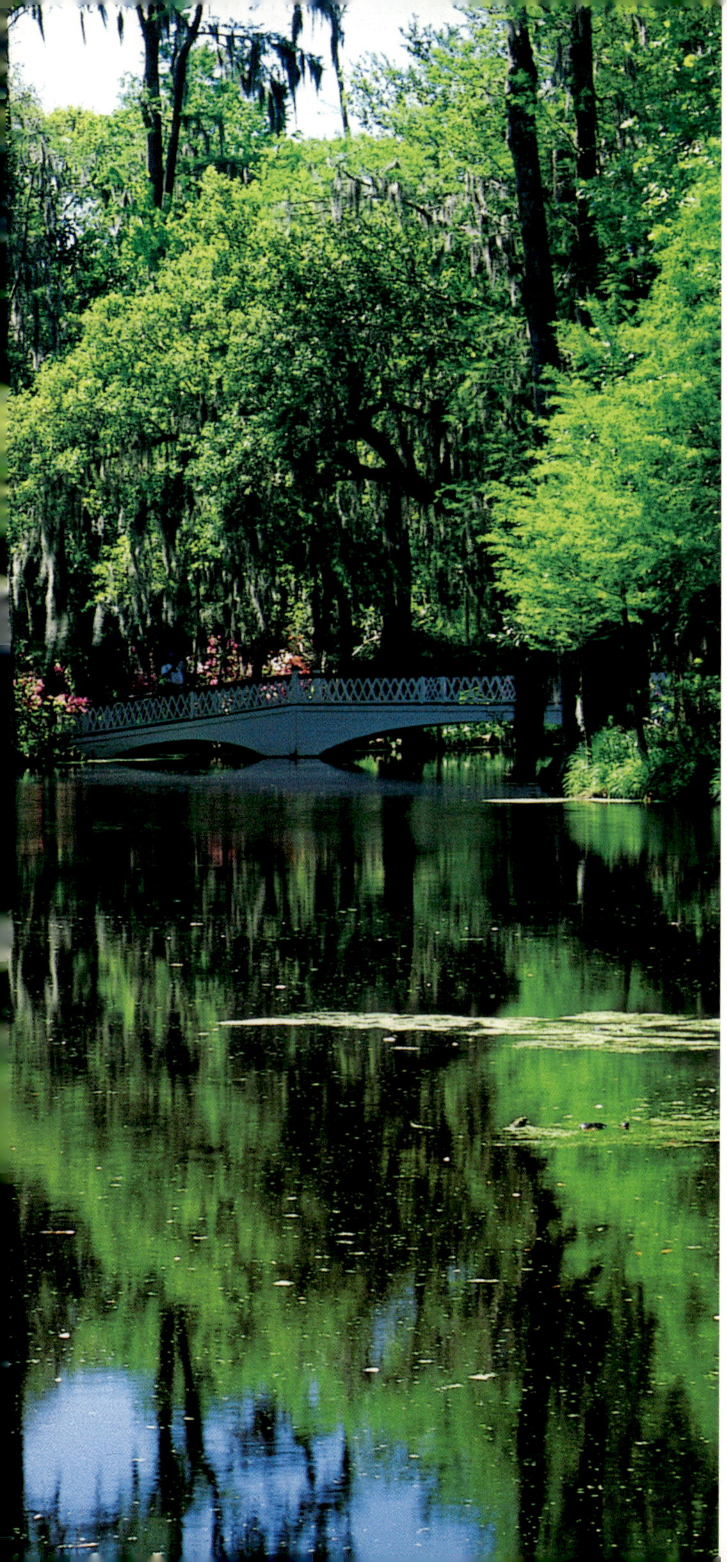

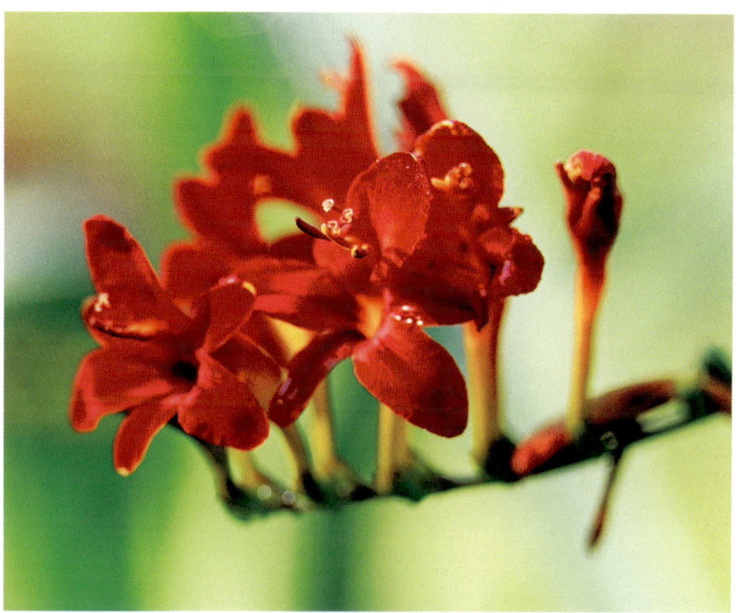

Above: Eye-catching crocosmia blooms at the South Carolina Botanical Garden. Designated the official state botanical garden in 1992, the 295-acre grounds in Clemson contain an eighteenth-century home, butterfly gardens, and an impressive collection of unusual and exotic plants. RON ANDERSON

Left: Founded in 1676, the Magnolia Plantation in Charleston is a South Carolina landmark. Pictured here is Audubon Swamp, a 60-acre blackwater swamp where more than 225 bird species have been documented, as well as many other wildlife varieties. RON ANDERSON

Facing page: Fred W. Symmes Chapel provides the spiritual centerpiece of YMCA Camp Greenville. The current chapel was constructed in 1941, and the camp itself—covering 1,600 acres—has been in existence since 1912. Ron Anderson

Below: Trinity Episcopal Cathedral in Columbia is modeled after England's York Minster and was consecrated in 1847. It miraculously escaped Sherman's wrath in 1865. Six state governors, eight bishops, and numerous Revolutionary and Civil War heroes are buried in the churchyard. Ron Anderson

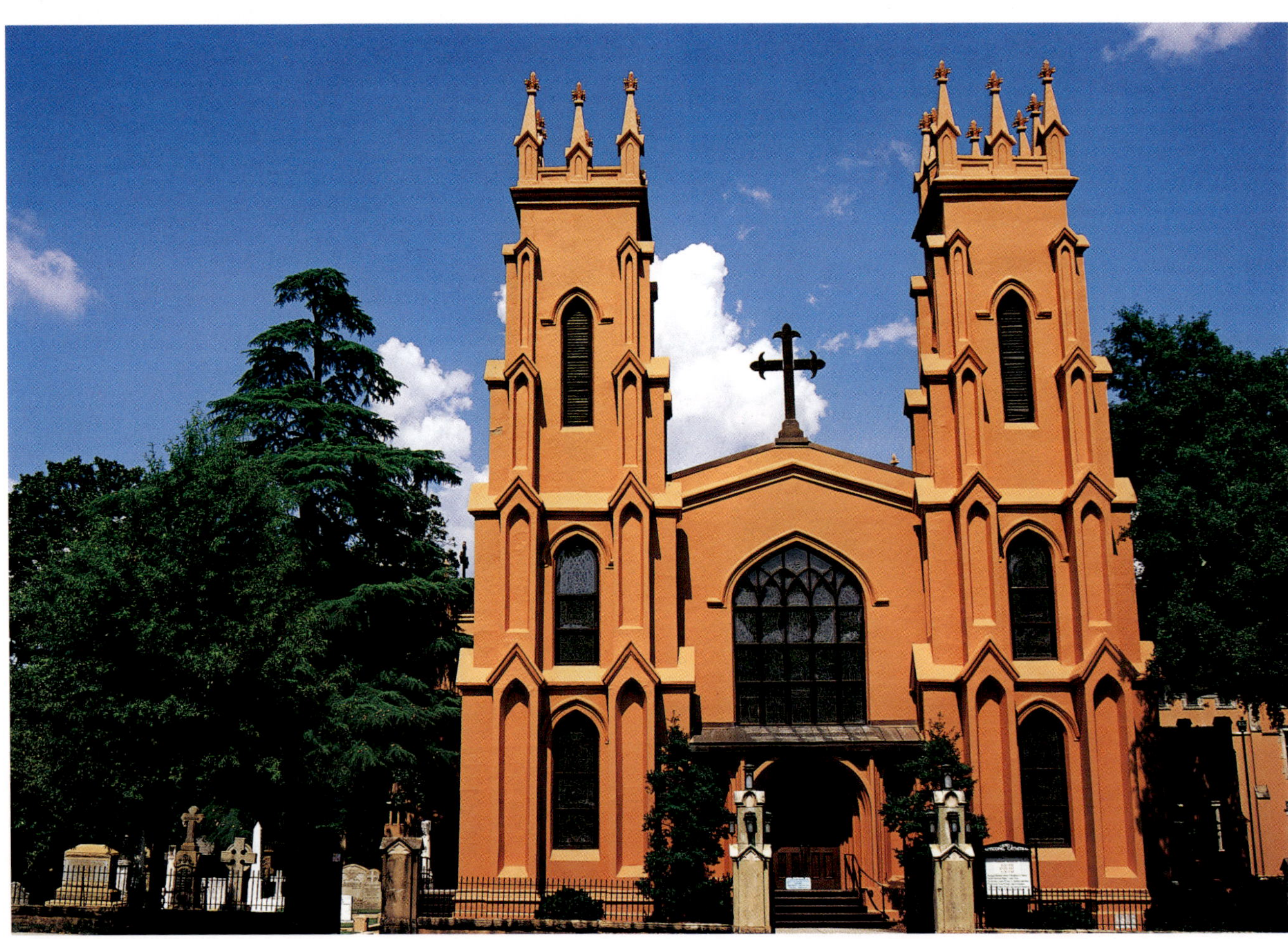

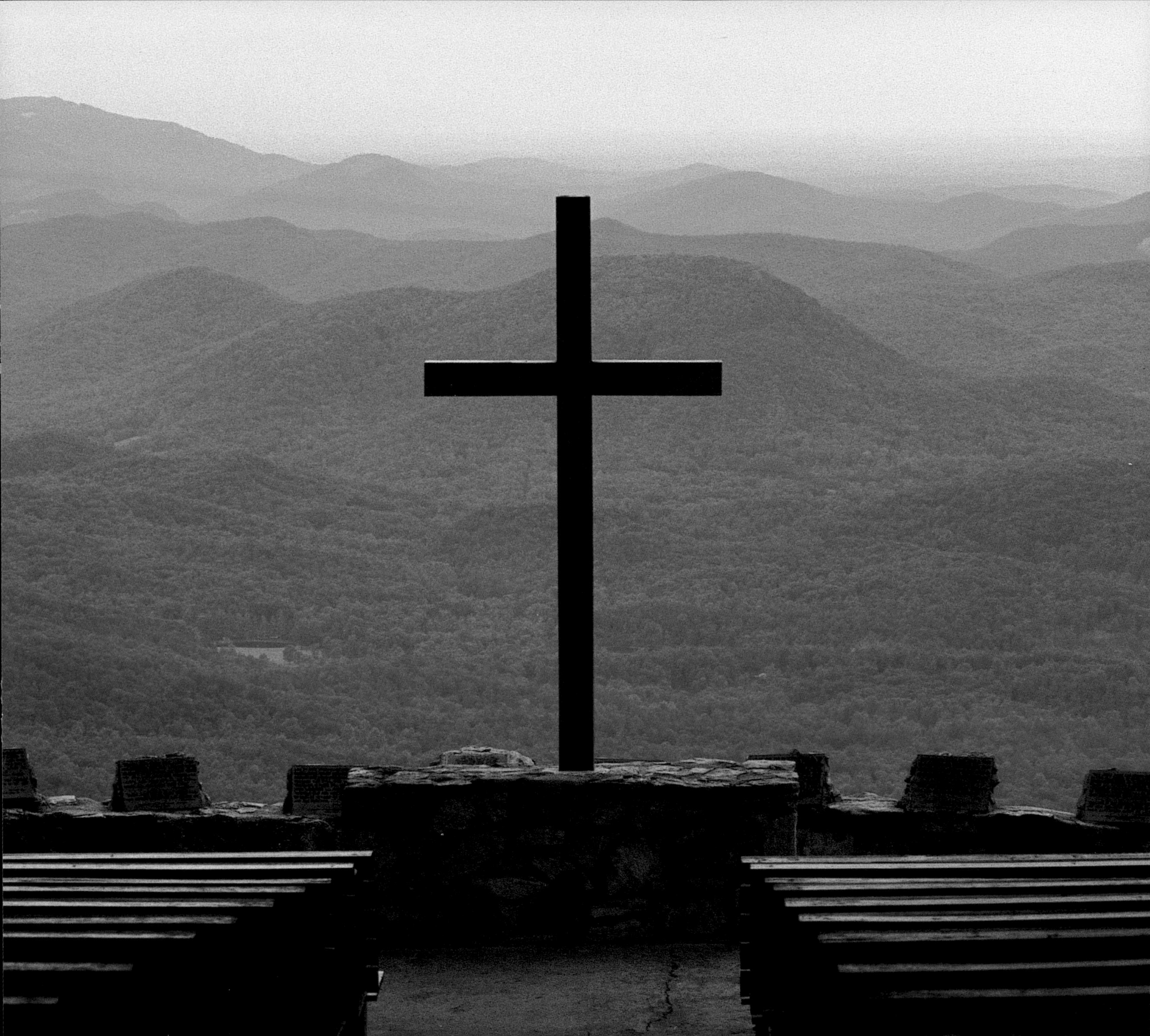

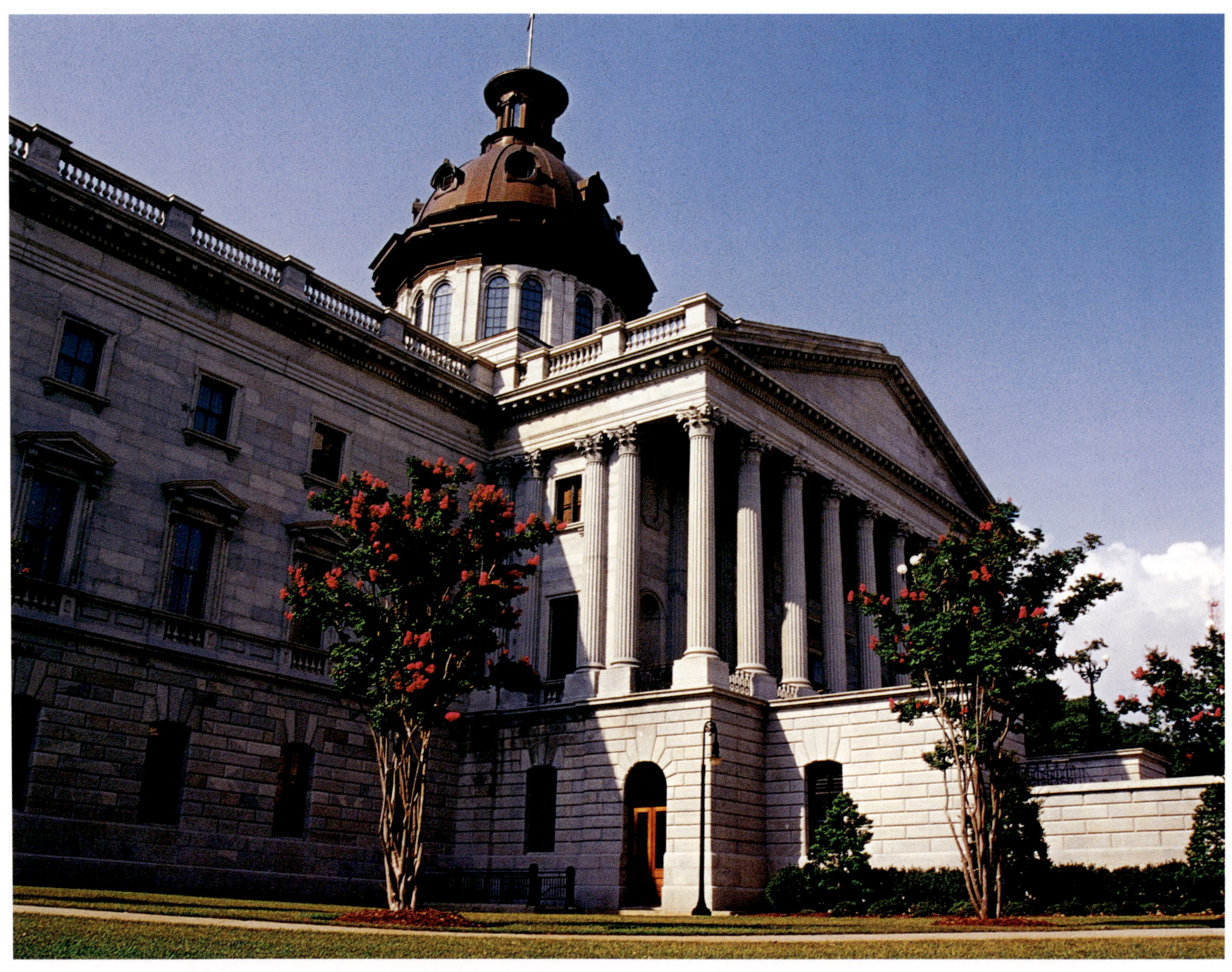

Above: The majestic State House that stands over Columbia was almost finished when the city was burned by Sherman's troops in 1865. For almost 20 years after the war, the building had a temporary roof, and it was the turn of the century before this noted historic treasure was finally completed. Ron Anderson

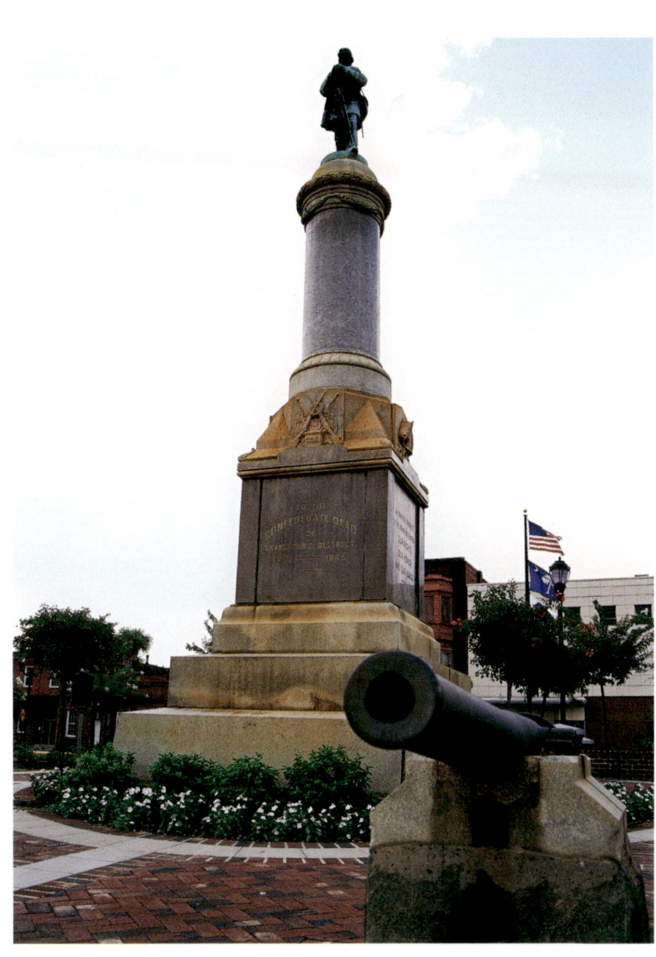

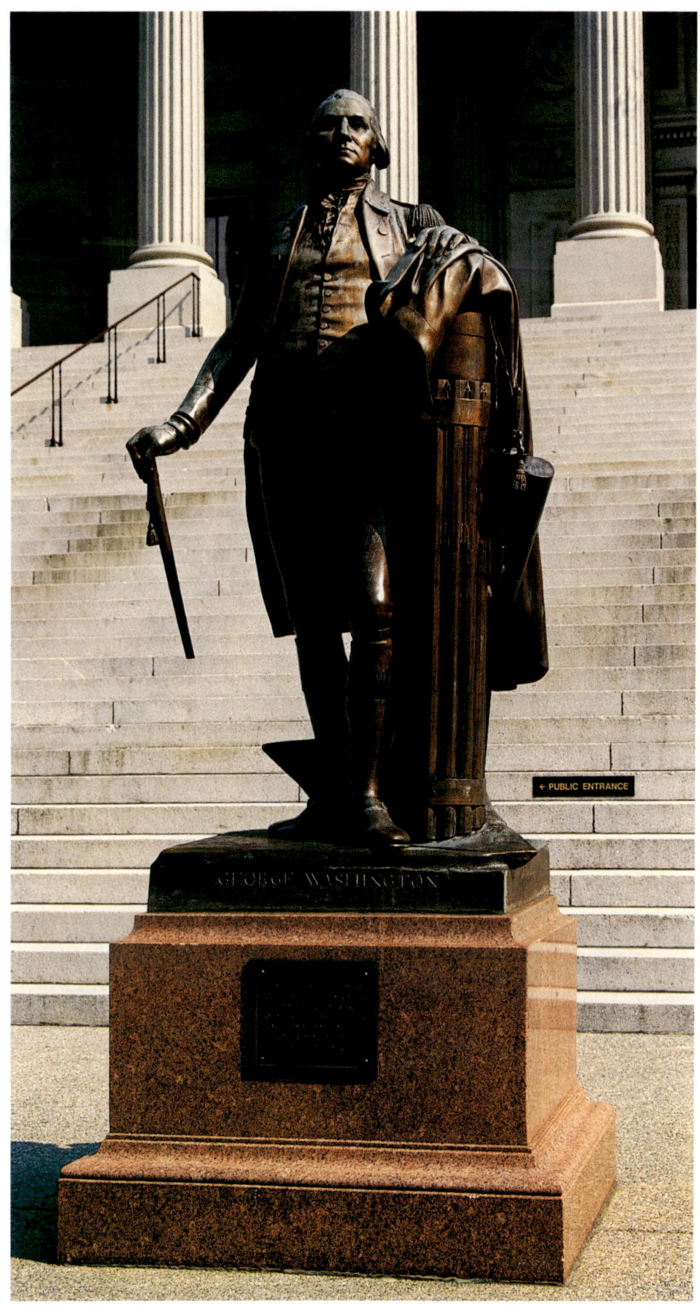

Above: A memorial to Confederate soldiers stands tall in Orangeburg. South Carolina lost a quarter of its white male population during the "War Between the States."
Ron Anderson

Right: A statue of our venerated first president adorns the State House grounds in Columbia. Ron Anderson

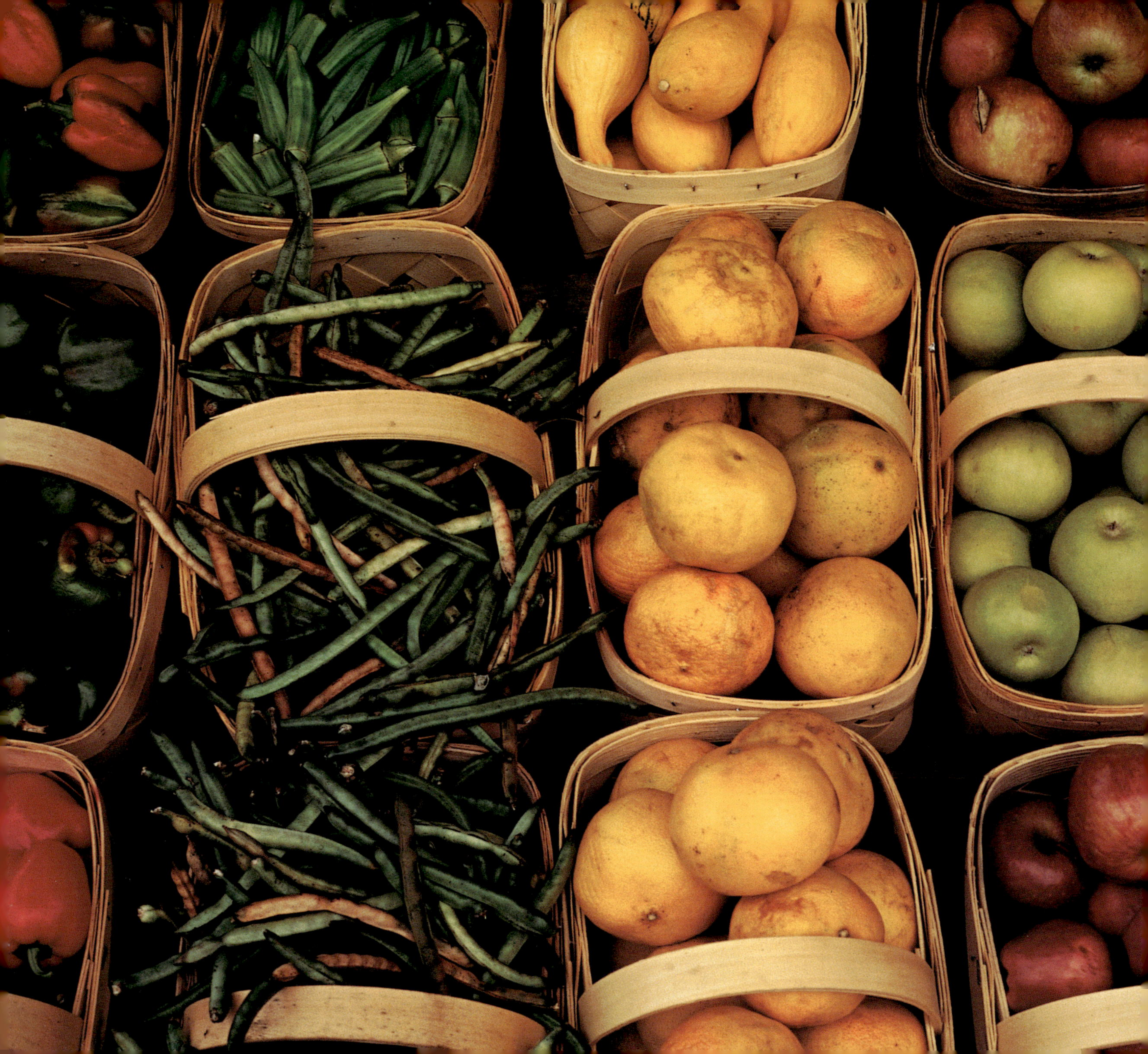

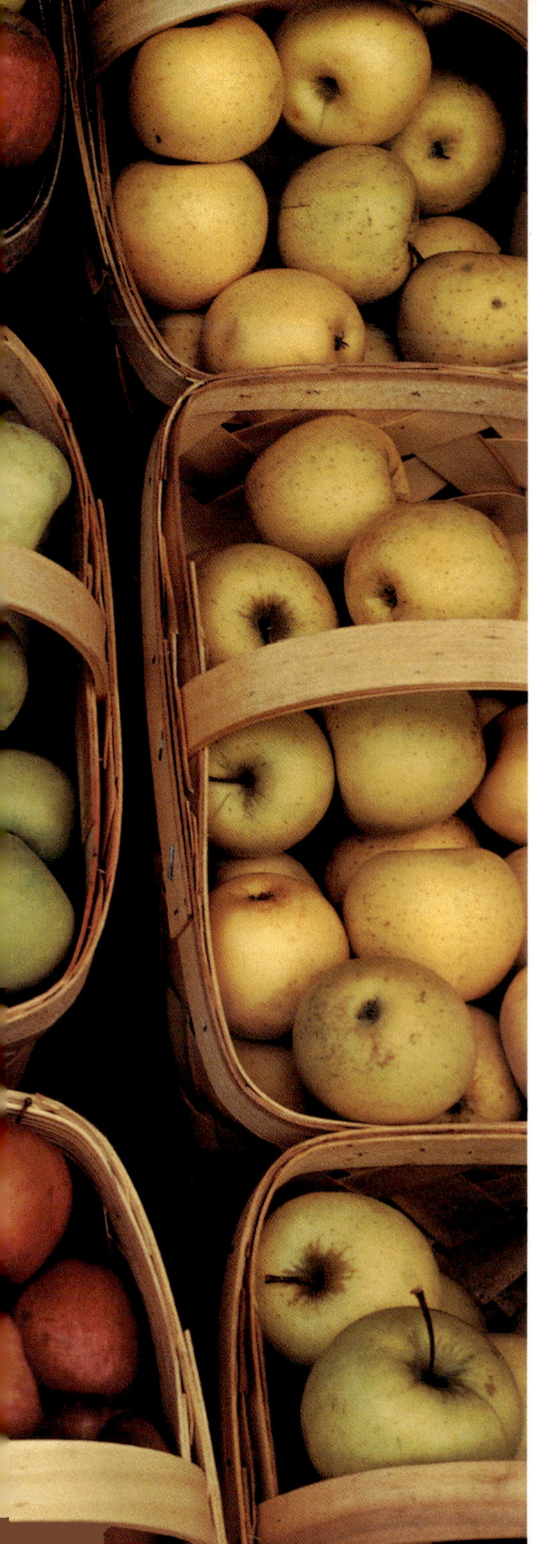

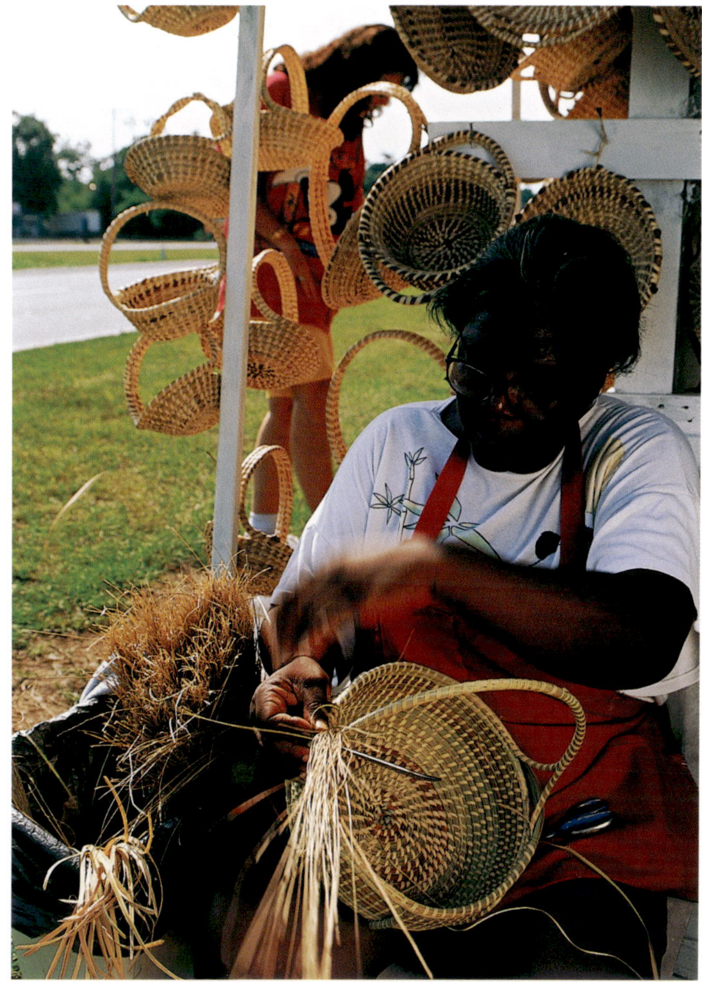

Above: A local craftswoman weaves baskets of sweetgrass. Most of these artfully crafted baskets are made by the Gullah, a people of African ancestry inhabiting the Sea Islands and the coastal areas of South Carolina, Georgia, and northern Florida. ERIC HORAN

Left: Wooden baskets of fresh produce entice hungry shoppers. South Carolina has a number of fine farmers' markets that attract many buyers in the summer months. ERIC HORAN

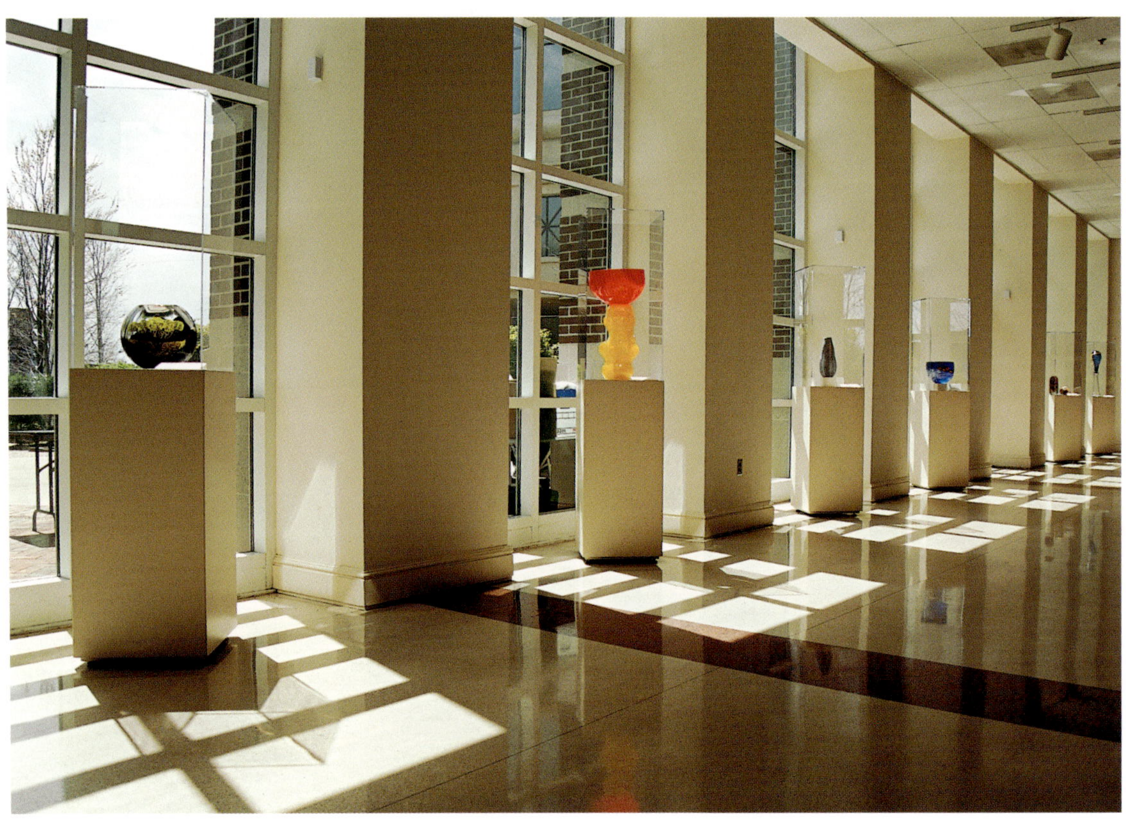

Above: The Columbia Museum of Art seeks to inspire, educate, and enrich with its large collection of art ranging from European Medieval treasures to contemporary glass sculptures. Originally opened in 1950, the museum moved to its new, expansive 20,000-square-foot facility in 1998. Ron Anderson

Right: Classical and cultural music presentations abound in South Carolina, which has produced opera singers Clara Louise Kellogg and Sarah Reese, as well as famous musicians "Whispering" Bill Anderson, James Brown, Chubby Checker, "Dizzy" Gillespie, Eartha Kitt, Edwin McCain, Linda Martell, Horace Ott, "Skipp" Pearson, Bill Pinkney, Myrtle Hall Smith, Angie Stone, and Aaron Tippen. This photograph was taken at the Spoleto Festival in Charleston. Eric Horan

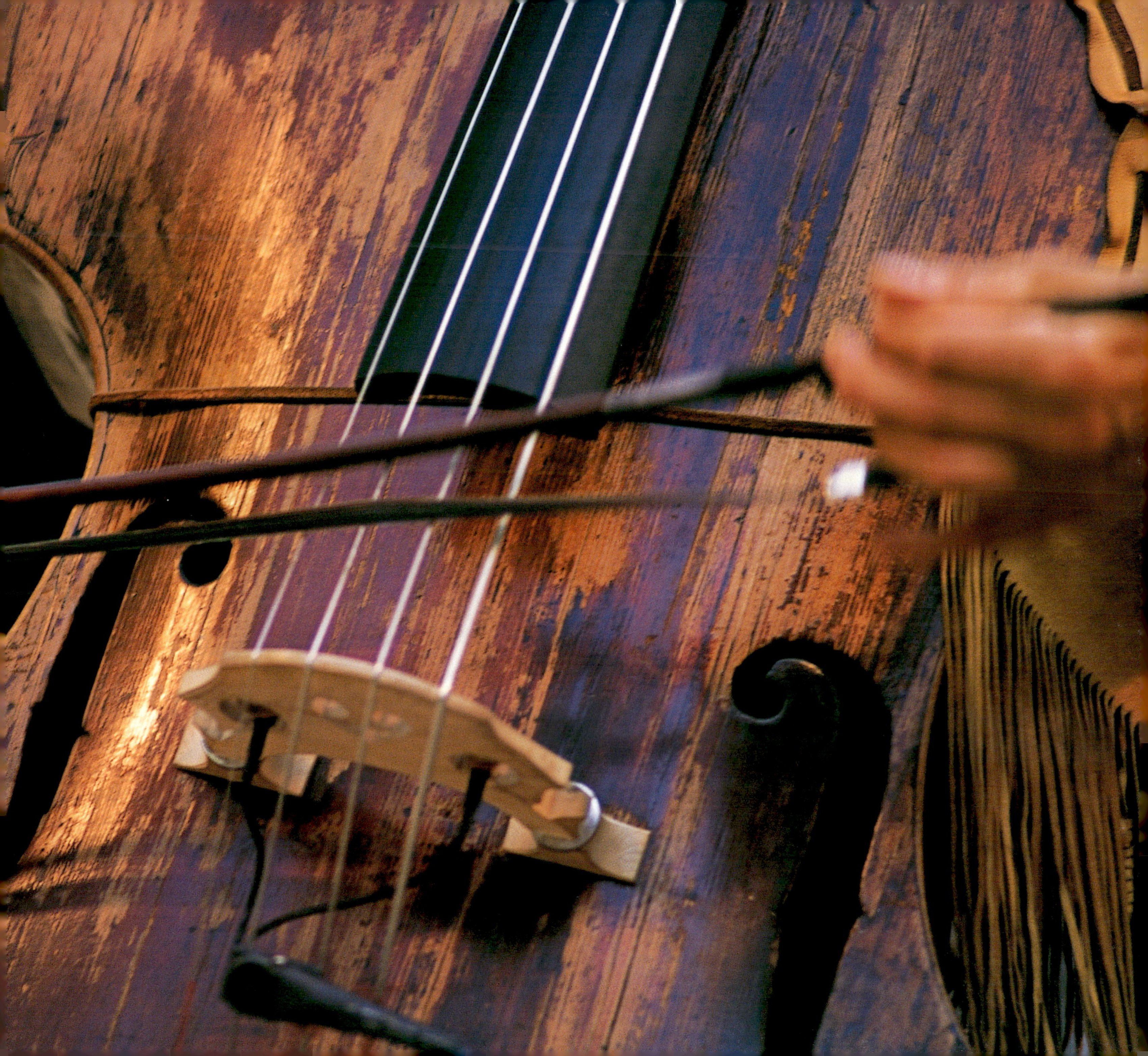

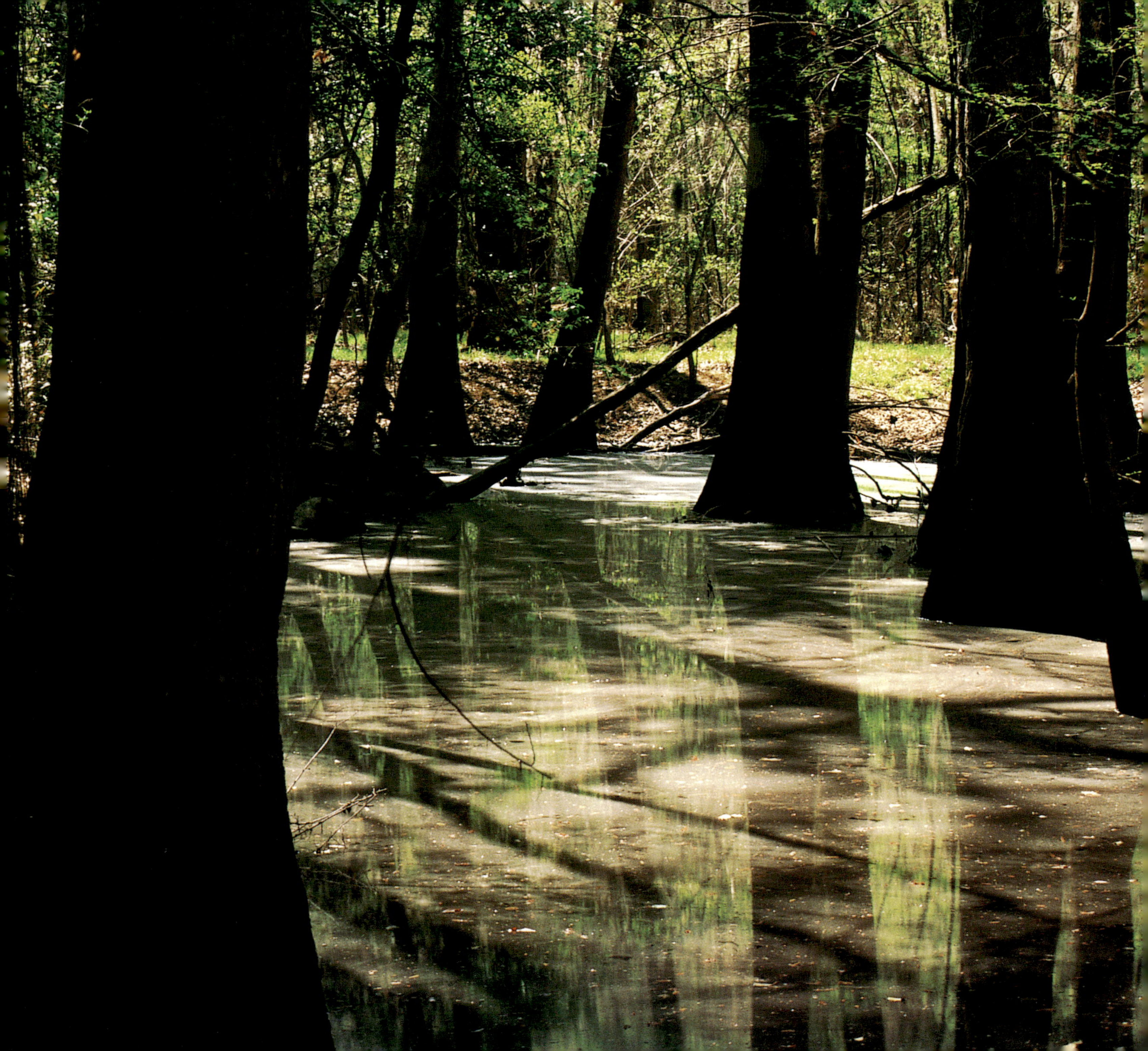

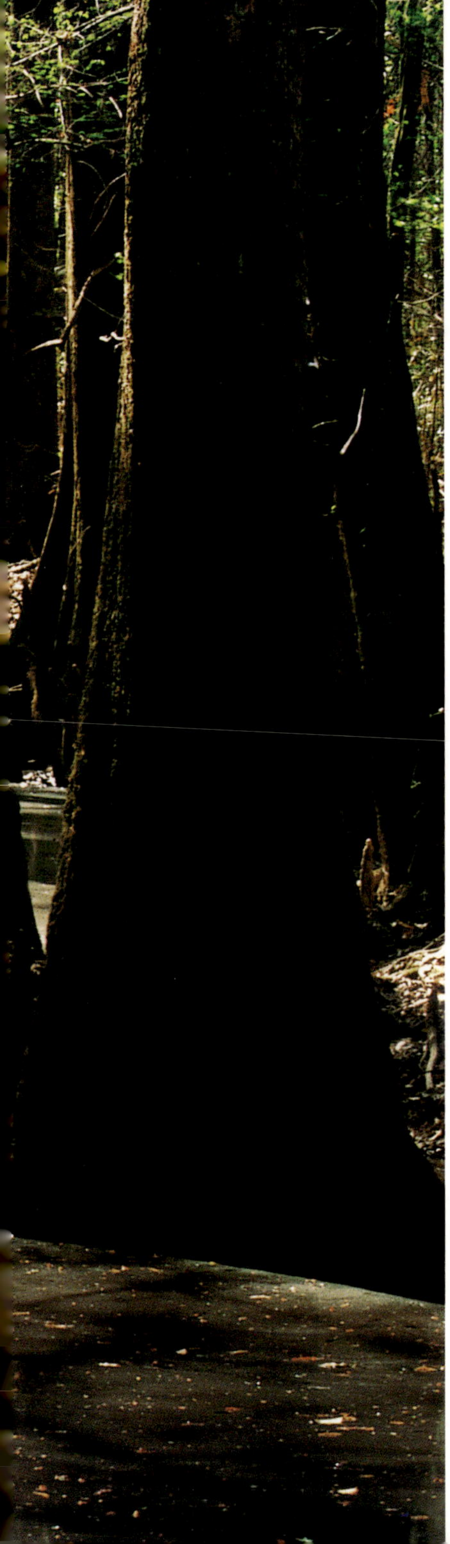

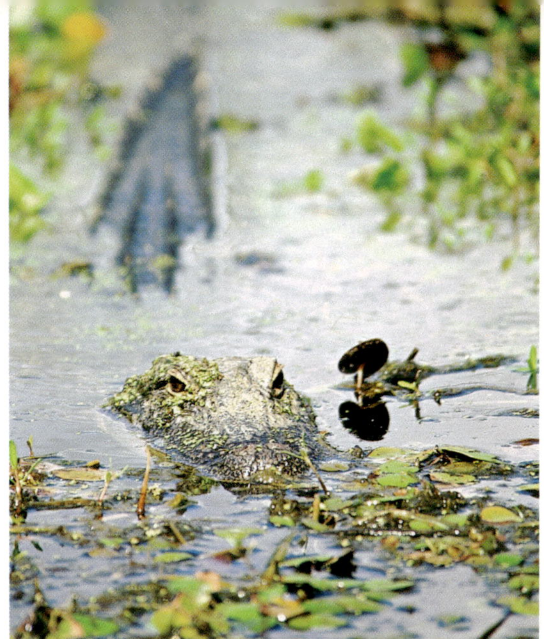

Left: An alligator might be spied around the Weston Lake area of Congaree National Park. Other plentiful wildlife in the park include feral hogs, deer, raccoons, snakes, turtles, crawfish, and many species of birds. RON ANDERSON

Far left: Bald cypress trees, known for their graceful fluted trunks and quirky "knees," are reflected in the still waters of the Congaree swamp. The area boasts approximately 90 tree species, many of record heights. RON ANDERSON

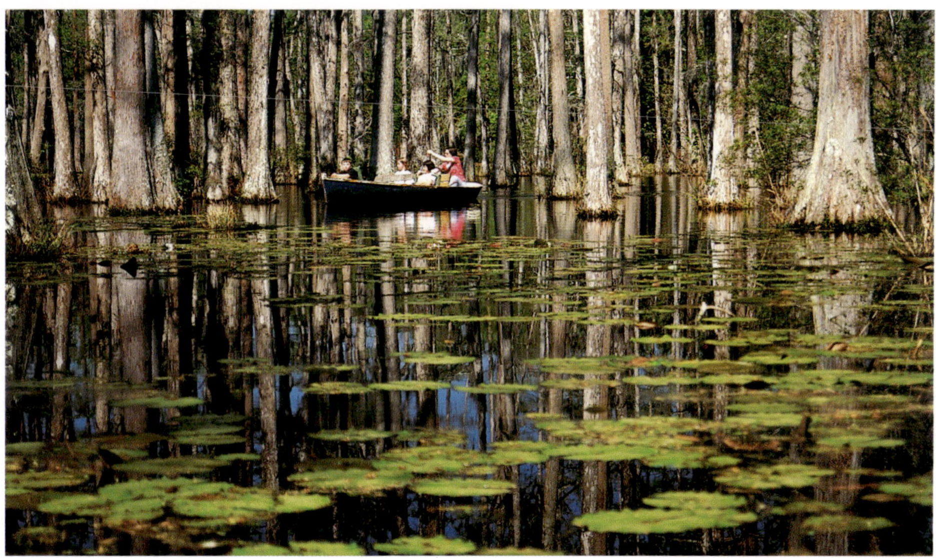

Above: A boat or canoe might be the best way to view the swamps of Congaree National Park, a name which honors the area's original inhabitants, the Congaree Indians. The park preserves 22,000 acres of old-growth floodplain forest in the Columbia area. Because of its unusual and rare flora and fauna, it is a designated International Biosphere Reserve. RON ANDERSON

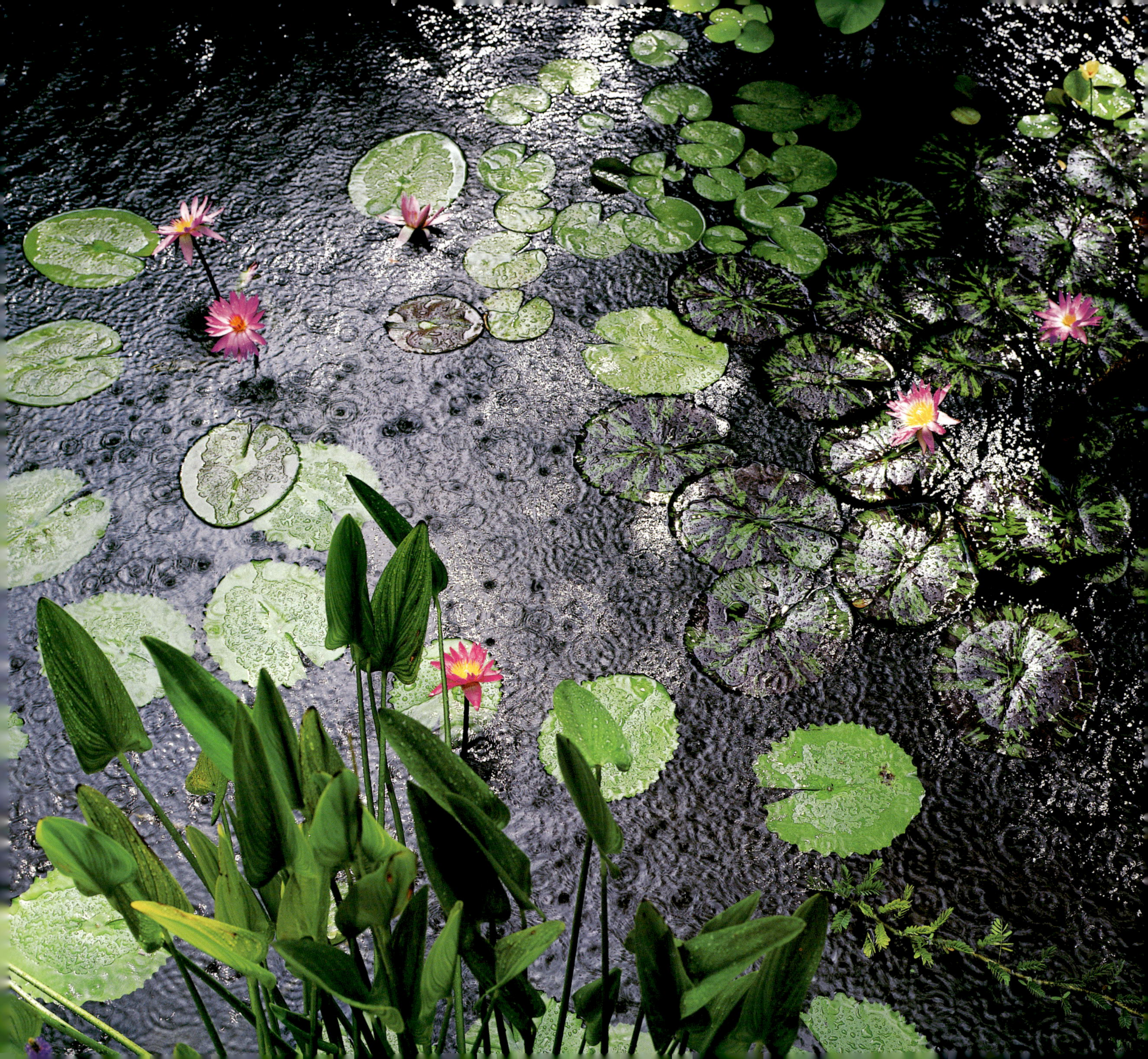

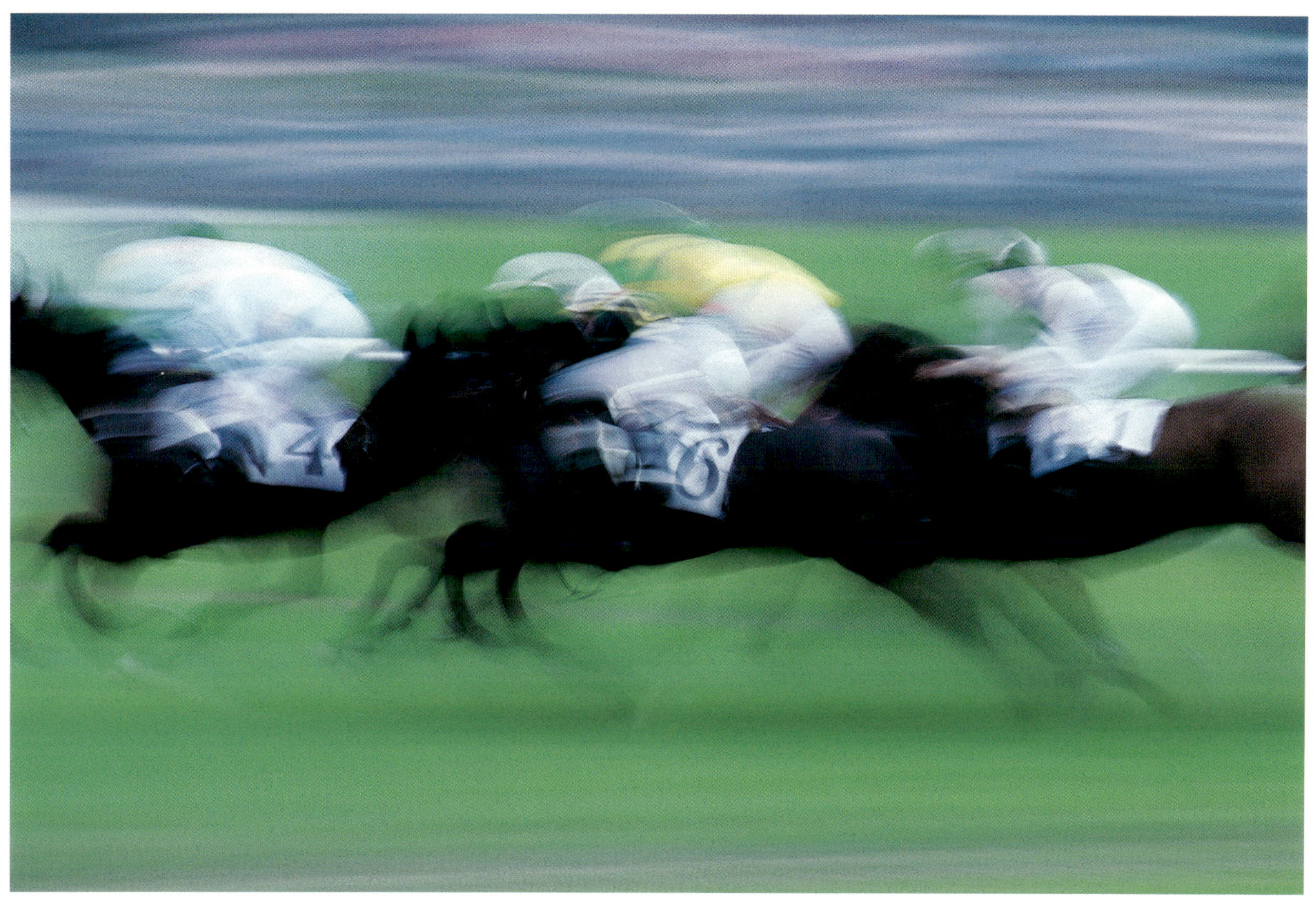

Above: Horseracing is a long-standing tradition in parts of South Carolina. Camden, for example, hosts several races of the steeplechase season, while Aiken has a history of polo. ERIC HORAN

Facing page: Water lilies drink in a summer rain. ERIC HORAN

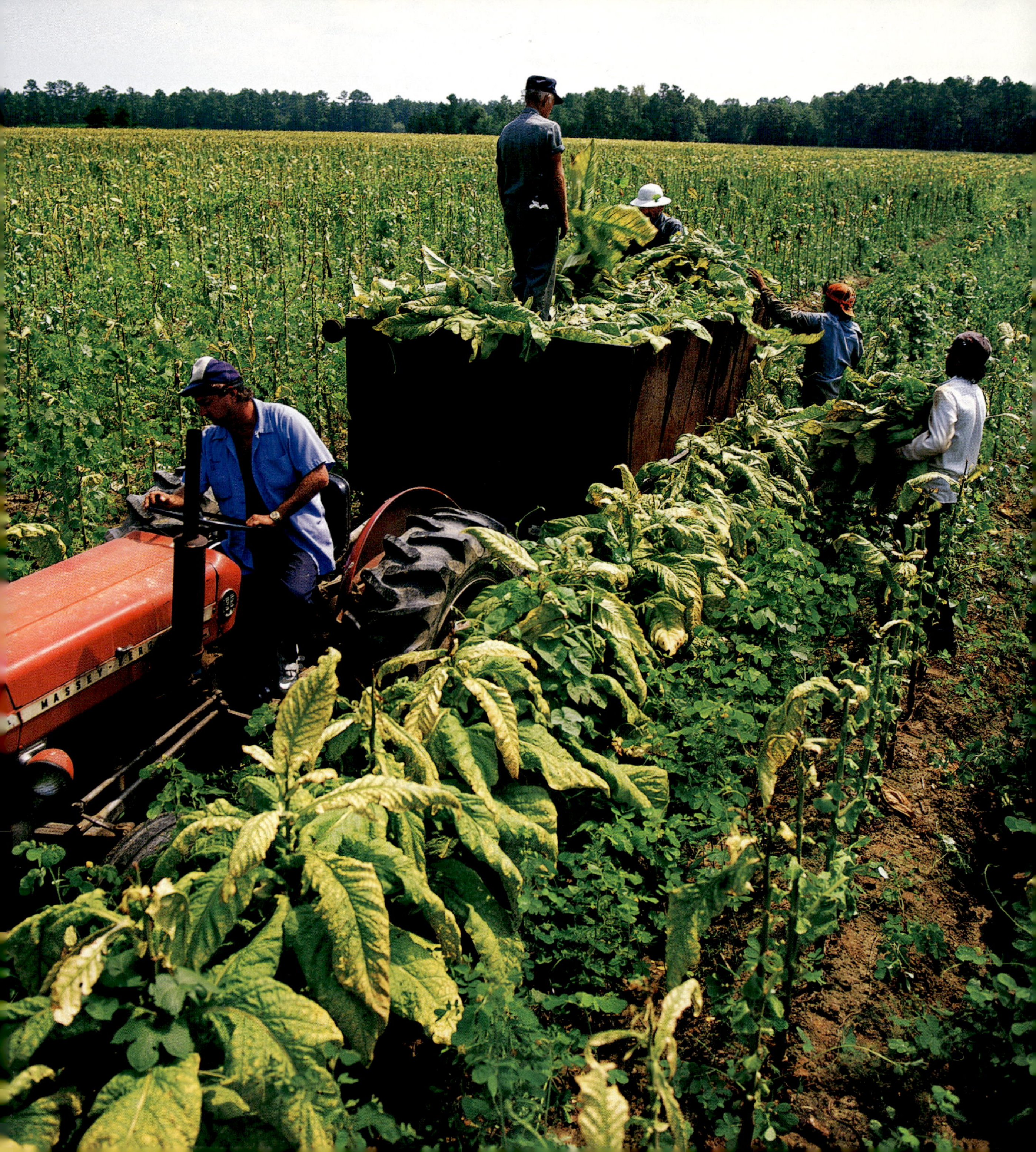

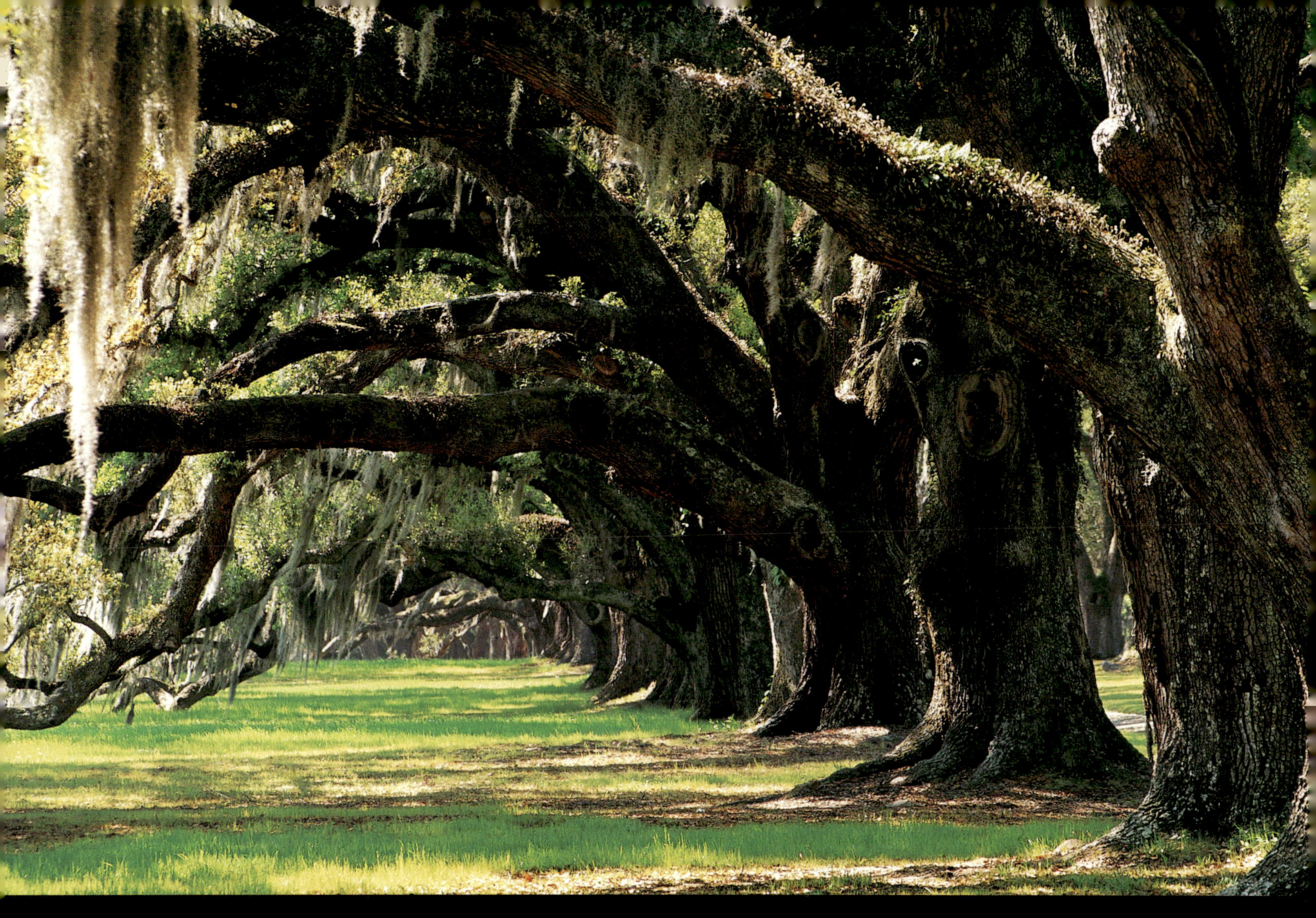

Above: The Avenue of the Oaks at the Tomotley Plantation in Sheldon showcases live oak and Spanish moss, two signature flora of the South Carolina landscape. Eric Horan

Facing page: Tobacco farming remains a staple of South Carolina agriculture. Eric Horan

Facing page: Peaches almost ripe for picking hang in heavy abundance in these orchards. South Carolina's $40-million peach season usually runs from the end of May through August. RON ANDERSON

Below: Recently added to the National Register of Historic Places, Senn's Grist Mill in Summerton is also a blacksmith shop and an Orange Crush bottling plant. ERIC HORAN

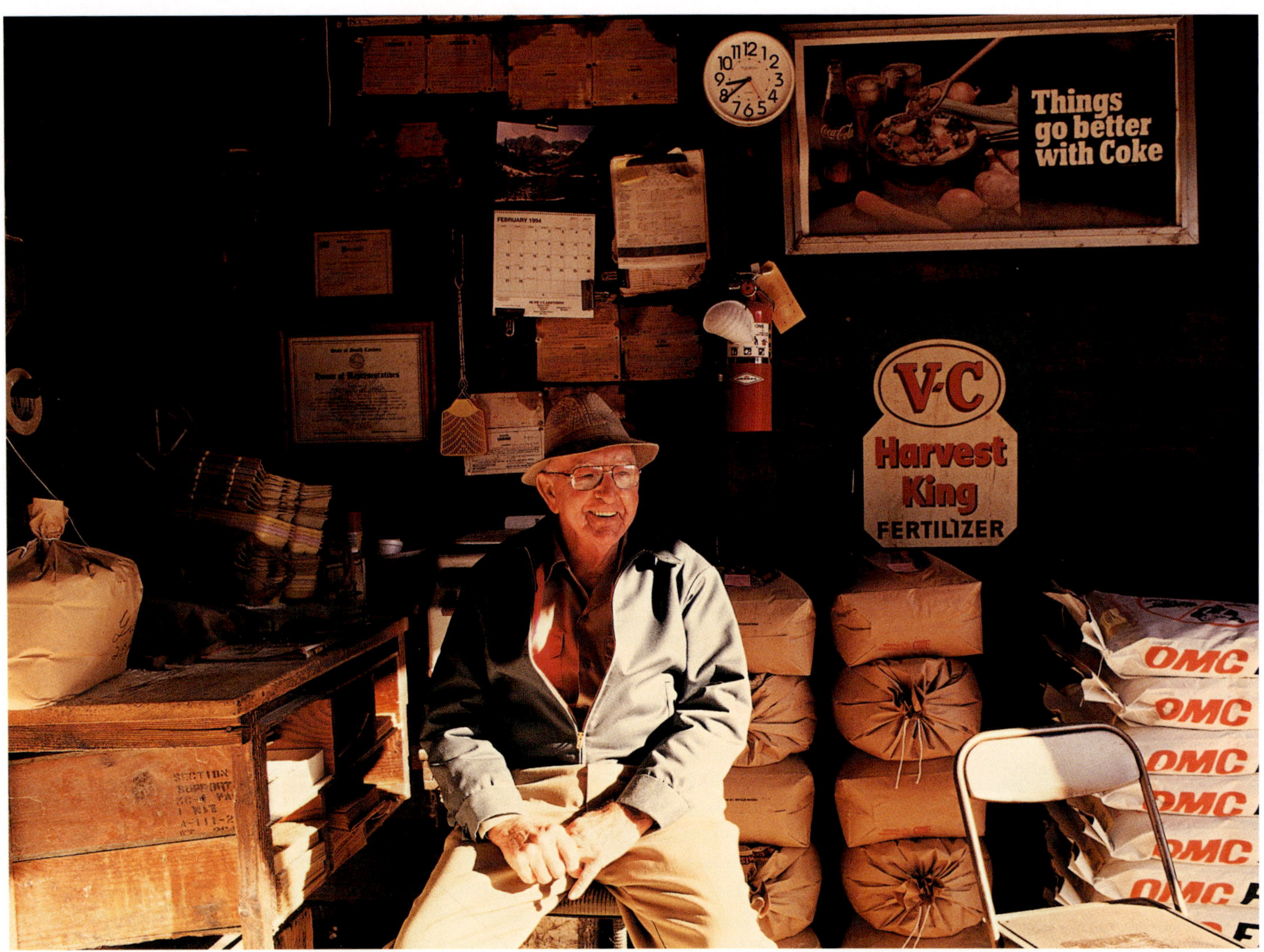

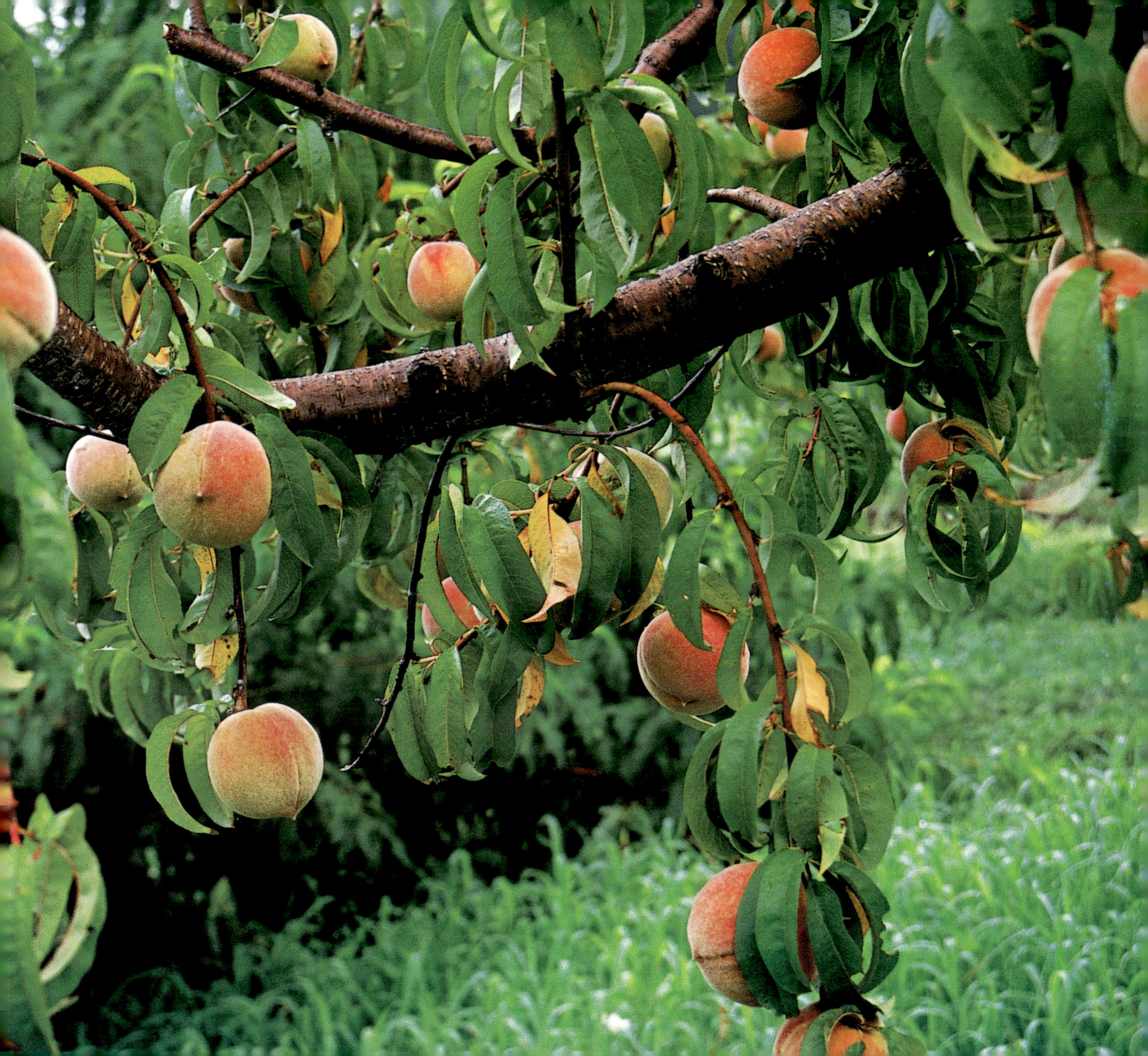

About the Photographers

Ron Anderson was born and raised in Easley, South Carolina, and has had an interest in photography since childhood. Ron quickly developed a seriousness and passion for the art and, with the encouragement of his wife, began entering local and national competitions. His photography has since been featured in publications such as the *Best of Photography Annual: 2002*, a scenic calendar produced for the Cradle of Forestry, and a special edition of a *Rand McNally Road Atlas*. His photography has also appeared in local galleries such as the Spartanburg County Museum of Art in Spartanburg and the DownTownes Gallery in Greenville. He soon realized that this passion he had been pursuing was actually a gift from God. "I couldn't know how to produce great images myself." He says, "It has to be a gift." Ron now lives in Campobello, South Carolina, with his wife, Miranda, their daughter, Rebekah, and their dog, Khaki. www.RonAndersonPhoto.com

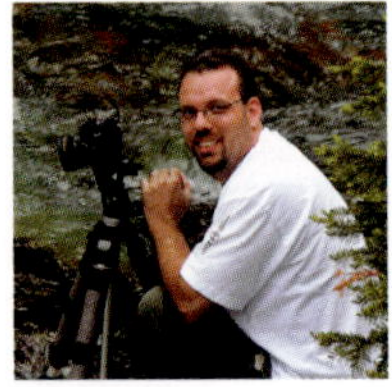

Eric Horan is a commercial photographer based in Beaufort, South Carolina. He graduated from the Colorado Mountain College in Glenwood Springs with a degree in commercial art and photography. His work includes fine art and assignment photography for both editorial and corporate clients, with extensive work in the resort market. He has been distinguished in national and international design competitions from notable sponsors: Carnegie Museum, Piccolo Spoleto Festival, *Studio Magazine, South Carolina Wildlife Magazine,* Timberpeg, and National Calendar Marketing Association. His photography has appeared in the books *South Carolina, A Compass American Guidebook, EXPOSURE,* 100 of *Outside Magazine's* finest photographs over 15 years, *Lowcountry A-Z,* and *National Geographic Books*. Eric's photography has appeared in such publications as *Business Week, Coastal Living, Cruising World, Fortune, McCall's,* Nature Conservancy's wall calendar, *New York Times Sunday Travel, Outside, Sail, Smithsonian, Tennis,* and *Time*. Eric's own publications include the coffee-table book *Carolina Nature* and three calendars, Lowcountry South Carolina, Hilton Head Island, South Carolina, and the Sea Islands of Georgia. www.southernlight.biz

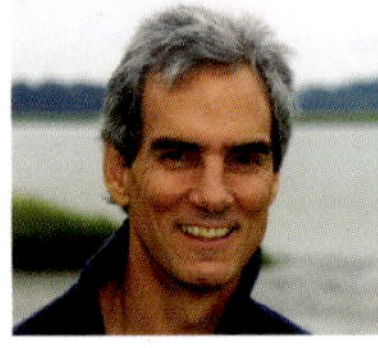

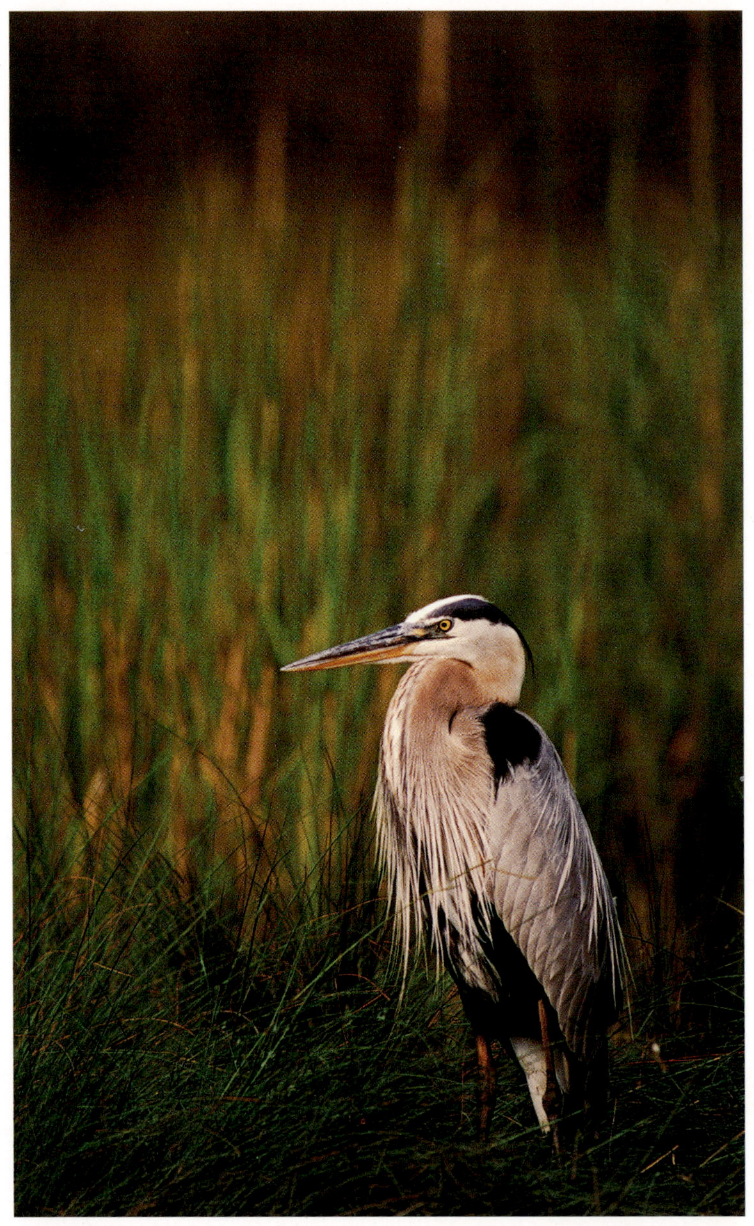

A blue heron surveys his surroundings, planning his next move.
Eric Horan